GW00361867

A TASTE OF MY WORLD

Morocco

Alaska

Thailand

To the wonderful women in my family – Mummy, Lyn and Samantha,

with love and thanks for being such great travelling companions

A TASTE OF MY WORLD

Katharine Pooley

A TASTE OF MY WORLD

Published by Pooleys Flight Equipment Limited
Mill Road, Cranfield
Beds
MK43 0JG
United Kingdom

~

Designed and produced by
S N P I N T E R N A T I O N A L
A division of SNP Media Asia Pte Ltd
491 River Valley Road
#01-19/20 Valley Point
Singapore 248371
Tel: (65) 6733 6163
Fax: (65) 6733 3671
snpinternational@snpcorp.com

Project Manager: Shova Loh
Creative Director & Photographer: Tuck Loong
Editor: Candice Chan
Photographer's Assistant: Winson Chua

~

© 2003 Katharine Pooley

Travel photographs kindly donated by
WADS, Patrick and Didi Wills, Michael Soucy, World Pictures, Besstock and Luca Tettoni
Food photography © 2003 Tuck Loong
Food styling by Sharon Soh and Amy Van, Sixth Sense Communications Pte Ltd
Crockery courtesy of Katharine Pooley and TANGS

Printed and bound by Antony Rowe Ltd, Eastbourne

ISBN 184 336 073 X

All proceeds from this cookbook will be donated equally to the following three charities:

• Future Hope based in India: provides street children of Calcutta with homes and education
• Tiger Tops based in Nepal: an international trust for nature conservation and the protection of tigers
• The Himalayan Trust based in Nepal: founded by Sir Edmund Hillary, this trust provides education, health services and
professional assistance to the Nepalese sherpas who climb among the high altitudes of the Himalayan mountains

LIFE JUST GIVES YOU TIME AND SPACE — IT'S UP TO YOU TO FILL IT

Katharine's house in Montebello, Hong Kong

Recipes – everyone has a favourite, everyone has experimented to create their own special dish.

A Taste of My World by Katharine Pooley shares her favourites and experiments. On her travels, she has collated many wonderful, unusual and tasty recipes from all over the world; the type that one just never gets to see or dares to ask for. Every recipe has its own story.

These easy-to-use recipes are good for simple lunches, or impressing guests at important dinner parties.

Hosting dinner parties at Katharine's home has become a part of life for her, and those who have attended will agree that everything from the table setting, the flowers, candles and the china to the beautifully presented, delicious food leaves guests with memories of a unique and inspired occasion.

But cooking is not just about sharing with friends and family, it is about the art of cooking and the enjoyment of being in the kitchen. Whatever your mood, enjoy this special cookbook and the fabulous travel photographs and memoirs that capture the exhilarating and adventurous world of Katharine Pooley, with dishes that indeed are worth staying home for.

My mother often reminds me that when I was all of 10 months old, she put me in the passenger seat of her Cessna aircraft and flew me off to foreign lands. It is here that my travels began.

My family has always had strong connections to the world of aviation, and from a young age my father encouraged us all to learn to fly, and to discover the wonderful mysteries and adventures that the world has to offer. It is therefore not surprising that travelling soon became a part of my everyday life.

It was also at an early stage in my life that I discovered an appreciation for the art of cooking. My stepmother Lyn, who loves to cook, spent time helping me understand the essential qualities of cooking, and showed me the important ingredients to creating a warm home.

I found that the more I travelled, the more I was tasting new and unique recipes, the majority of which were from private families. I soon began to collect them with a passion.

It has now been over 28 years since I started collecting recipes from all corners of the globe, and finally, after much encouragement and support from Rob and my family, I decided to publish this travel cookbook containing not only recipes but some of my travel experiences and photographs.

Many of these recipes bring to life old classics, with enhanced flavours and delightfully different textures. If it is success you are looking for, I have only one kitchen rule: it is important to take pleasure in every recipe and it is paramount that if you wish to get a perfect result, you must cook each dish with love!

I would like to take this opportunity to thank everyone who has been generous in sharing their recipes with me. I hope they will be enjoyed and appreciated throughout the world, bringing as much pleasure to others as they have to me.

To cook and to be cooked for is one of the most precious experiences in life. I hope this book helps that happen for you...

Katharine Pooley

MY FAVOURITE RECIPES

CANAPÉS & STARTERS

Hong Kong

Lily Ahn's Black and Green Olive Canapés

1 can (1 pound/450 g) black olives

1 can (1 pound/450 g) green olives

2 bottles (^{1}/$_2$ pound/225 g) sun-dried tomatoes

5 stalks English parsley

zest and juice of 1 lemon

3 tablespoons olive oil

1 French baguette

butter

Finely chop the black and green olives, sun-dried tomatoes, parsley and lemon zest. Mix with olive oil and lemon juice.

Slice the bread thinly, toast with a little butter. Spread the olive mixture on top and serve.

Lily Ahn's Hot Crab Dip

This recipe and the previous one were given to me by Lily Ahn from Hong Kong. She is undoubtedly one of the most fantastic hostesses I know, always throwing the best parties. Apart from her gorgeous designer house, her canapés are to die for. My favourite is this Hot Crab Dip. Once you have taken a mouthful, you just won't be able to stop.

Makes 3^1/$_2$ cups.

3 tablespoons unsalted butter

2 medium shallots, minced

1 tablespoon water

^{1}/$_4$ teaspoon cayenne pepper

^{3}/$_4$ teaspoon Old Bay seasoning

1^1/$_2$ teaspoons dry mustard

^{3}/$_4$ cup half-and-half (made up of equal parts cream and milk)

8 ounces/225 g cream cheese, cut into small pieces

4 ounces/110 g white Cheddar cheese, grated on the large holes of a box grater to yield 1^3/$_4$ cups

3 tablespoons fresh lemon juice

2 teaspoons Lea & Perrins Worcestershire sauce

10 ounces/280 g crabmeat, picked over for cartilage

^{1}/$_2$ cup chopped fresh flat-leaf parsley

2 slices white bread, crusts removed, torn into ^{1}/$_4$-inch pieces

^{1}/$_2$ teaspoon paprika

Preheat the oven to 400°F/200°C/Gas 6 with the rack in the centre. Melt 2 tablespoons of the butter in a medium saucepan over medium heat. Add the shallots and cook until soft, about 2 minutes. Add 1 tablespoon water and simmer for 30 seconds. Stir in the cayenne, Old Bay and dry mustard until well combined. Pour the half-and-half into the saucepan and bring to a simmer.

Slowly whisk in the cream cheese, a few pieces at a time. When the cream cheese is fully incorporated, whisk in

Lily Ahn's Hot Crab Dip

the Cheddar cheese a bit at a time. Stir the mixture for 2 minutes. Remove from the heat. Add the lemon juice and Worcestershire sauce and stir to combine. Add the crabmeat and half the parsley and stir.

Transfer the mixture to an ovenproof baking dish and sprinkle with the bread pieces and the remaining tablespoon of butter. Sprinkle with the paprika. Bake for 18 to 22 minutes, until the bread pieces are golden and the dip is hot. Garnish with the remaining parsley and serve with crudités, bread sticks, crisps or toast.

Vegetable Spring Rolls

Vegetable Spring Rolls

Having spent over 12 years living in Hong Kong and one year in Vietnam, I love Asian food. Here is a selection of my favourite spring roll recipes. Most of them come from a divine little restaurant in Hanoi called Lemongrass.

oil for frying

1 onion, sliced

3/4 ounce/20 g glass noodles

2 ounces/50 g cabbage, shredded

1 carrot, shredded

1 bell pepper, shredded

1 teaspoon soy sauce

salt to taste

pinch of sugar

pinch of white pepper

6 spring roll sheets

1 egg, beaten, to seal rolls

Chicken Vegetable Spring Rolls

Heat a little of the oil in a saucepan and sauté the sliced onion. Add the glass noodles, shredded cabbage, carrot and bell pepper. Stir in the soy sauce and seasoning.

Open out a spring roll sheet and add 3/4 –1 ounce/20–30 g filling. Roll tightly from corner to corner, folding in the other two opposite corners about half-way through rolling. Seal the free end with egg. Fry rolls in hot oil till golden brown.

TIP: Add boiled and shredded chicken for chicken spring rolls.

Chicken Vegetable Spring Rolls

1 thinly sliced onion

2 tablespoons vegetable oil

1 cup shredded carrots

1 cup shredded sweet red bell pepper

salt or fish sauce for seasoning

1/2 cup chopped coriander leaves

2 cups shredded roast chicken

shredded fresh crunchy lettuce

spring roll wrappers

Dip: Thai sweet chilli sauce

Sauté the onion with vegetable oil for one minute. Add the carrots and red bell pepper and stir-fry for 5 minutes. Season with salt or fish sauce, then add the chopped coriander. Stir-fry, then remove from heat and leave to cool. Wrap the shredded chicken with the vegetables and shredded fresh lettuce in spring roll wrappers. Serve with Thai sweet chilli sauce.

21

Classic Vietnamese Spring Rolls

FILLING

1/2 pound/225 g ground pork

2 ounces/50 g peeled and deveined medium shrimp, briefly rinsed and finely chopped (about 1/2 cup)

1/2 medium onion (or 1 large shallot), finely chopped

2 cloves garlic, minced

2 to 3 shallots, minced

1/2 cup finely chopped jicama (Mexican turnip/potato, a leguminous root) or carrot (optional)

1 ounce/30 g cellophane noodles, soaked in warm water for 20 minutes, drained, and cut into 1 inch/ 2 1/2 cm lengths with scissors (just over 1/2 cup)

1/4 teaspoon freshly ground black pepper

2 tablespoons Vietnamese fish sauce

40 small round rice papers (about 5 inches/ 13 cm across) or wedge-shaped papers, or substitute ten 8 inch/20 cm round rice papers

peanut oil for deep-frying

To make the filling, place the pork in a medium bowl, add all the other filling ingredients, and mix very well. You will have about 2 cups of filling. Set aside. (You can prepare this ahead and store in a well-sealed container in the refrigerator for up to 12 hours.)

Vietnam

Set out two large plates or a flat tray. Wet a tea towel well, then wring out and place on your work surface. Fill a wide bowl or basin with 2 inches/5 cm of warm water. (Or fill with 1 inch/2 1/2 cm beer and add 1 inch/2 1/2 cm hot water, to make a warm mixture.)

If using small round papers or wedges, immerse a sheet in the warm soaking liquid until well softened, then lay on the damp tea towel (place the wedge with the point facing away from you). Place a generous teaspoon of the filling onto the paper in a 2 inch/5 cm long line near and parallel to the round edge nearest you. Roll that edge over the filling, then fold over the sides of the rice paper and roll up tightly. Place the finished roll on

the plate or tray, seam side down, and cover with a damp cloth. Repeat for the remaining rolls.

If using large papers, wet one paper thoroughly until softened, then place on the damp tea towel. Place a scant 2 table-spoons filling in a line about 5 inches/ 13 cm long across the wrapper, well below the midline, leaving a 3/4 inch/ 2 cm gap at either end of the line. Fold the edge nearest you over the filling, fold in the sides, and roll up tightly. Place on the plate or tray, cover with a damp cloth, and repeat with the remaining papers and filling.

TIP: Serve with Thai sweet chilli sauce.

Vietnam… The word conjures up images of lively people, bustling around in their daily grind. The population is about 80 million, and it seems as if everybody goes around on two wheels. The roads are full of cyclists, including women in gloves, beautiful hats and *ao dai*, the demure Vietnamese long-sleeved, high-necked, calf-length tunic worn over trousers, looking as if they're going to the opera instead of just making their way to work. Everyone is talking, laughing – and eating.

Vietnam was a French colony from 1883 until just after the Second World War, and while the cooking techniques reveal China's impact, the Gallic influence is evident in Vietnamese food. It was the French, for example, who introduced the beef found in *pho*, the popular Vietnamese noodle soup, to a traditionally pork-eating people. (By the way, *pho ga* means you'll get chicken in the soup, while *pho bo* is beef.) One clue to its origin is the fact that *pho* is pronounced exactly like the French *feu*, or fire. Other borrowed ingredients are butter and cheese.

A dear friend, Didi, and I had just stepped out of a restaurant in Ho Chi Minh City, after enjoying hearty bowls of *pho*, fragrant with fresh basil, spring onion and coriander leaves, when we spotted a tiny kitten on the pavement. It looked so pathetically hungry that we just had to go back into the restaurant and order another dish to feed it. The waiter was astonished, but the food was cooked and we brought it out to the kitten, who began disposing of it as fast as it could. The sight of two apparently mad Englishwomen feeding a stray seemed to be a rare occurrence, going by the crowd that gathered to watch the kitten eating.

Yet this was nothing compared to the 140,000 children who have received aid from the Christina Noble Children's Foundation. Christina Noble, who grew up a street child in her native Ireland, arrived in Vietnam in 1989. She set up the foundation in Vietnam and Mongolia, with the mission of providing medicine and education for underprivileged children and their families. Using my network as the manager of a business centre in Hong Kong, I canvassed for donations of funds, clothes, medicine and toys from numerous businesses with offices in Asia, including OshKosh and Watson's. Christina Noble is an inspiration to us all, and I count myself fortunate in having been able to help her cause in Vietnam.

Crab Cakes

I've eaten many versions of crab cakes at cocktail parties but these are simply delicious. Originally, this recipe came from the Hamptons, but it has been slightly modified to suit my own taste. This is always the first appetiser to go at a party.

Serves 6 to 8.

2 tablespoons unsalted butter

2 tablespoons olive oil

3/4 cup small-diced red onion (1 small onion)

1 1/2 cups small-diced celery (4 stalks)

1/2 cup small-diced red bell pepper (1 small pepper)

1/2 cup small-diced yellow bell pepper (1 small pepper)

1/4 cup minced fresh flat-leaf parsley

1 tablespoon capers, drained

1/4 teaspoon Tabasco sauce

1/2 teaspoon Lea & Perrins Worcestershire sauce

1 1/2 teaspoons Old Bay seasoning (do not substitute if you cannot find this)

1/2 teaspoon salt

1/2 teaspoon freshly ground black pepper

1/2 pound/225 g crabmeat, drained and picked to remove shells

1/2 cup plain dry breadcrumbs

1/2 cup good mayonnaise

2 teaspoons Dijon mustard

2 extra large eggs, lightly beaten

FOR FRYING

4 tablespoons unsalted butter

1/4 cup olive oil

Place the butter, oil, onion, celery, red and yellow bell peppers, parsley, capers, Tabasco sauce, Worcestershire sauce, Old Bay seasoning, salt and pepper in a large sauté pan over medium-low heat and cook until the vegetables are soft, about 15 to 20 minutes. Cool to room temperature.

In a large bowl, break the crabmeat into small pieces and toss with the bread-crumbs, mayonnaise, mustard and eggs. Add the cooked mixture and mix well. Cover and chill in the refrigerator for 30 minutes. Shape into bite-sized crab cakes.

Heat the butter and olive oil for frying over medium heat in a large sauté pan. Add the crab cakes and fry for 4 to 5 minutes on each side, until browned. Drain on paper towels; keep them warm in a 250°F/120°C/Gas 1 oven and serve hot.

TIP: Crab cakes can be shaped and stored overnight in the fridge on baking sheets wrapped in plastic. Fry just before serving with rémoulade sauce (recipe follows).

RÉMOULADE SAUCE

Makes 3/4 cup.

1/2 cup mayonnaise

2 tablespoons small-diced pickles or cornichons

1 teaspoon coarse-grained mustard

1 tablespoon champagne or white wine vinegar

pinch of salt

pinch of pepper

Put all the ingredients in a food processor fitted with a steel blade and pulse several times until the pickles are finely chopped and all the ingredients are well mixed but not puréed.

Sri Lanka

Linda's Black Olive and Corn Dip

This is a very simple and easy recipe for light and casual entertaining – perfect with a glass of wine at the end of a hard day.

8 ounces/225 g cream cheese

10 ounces/280 g carton sour cream

half a 1¹/₂ ounce/40 g packet of fresh onion soup mix

4¹/₂ ounce/125 g can corn kernels, drained

7 ounces/200 g packet corn crisps or potato chips, crushed

2 black olives

Beat the soft cream cheese in a small bowl until smooth. Beat in the sour cream and soup mix and stir in the corn kernels, corn crisps/potato chips and black olives until creamy smooth. Place the mixture in a bowl and serve with corn crisps or crudités.

Avocado Mousse

I first tasted this recipe in Verbier – incredibly simple and fast to make but very effective for a dinner party when served in small ramekin dishes. You just need to be careful not to prepare too far in advance as the avocados will turn brown.

2 ripe avocados

1 packet of Philadelphia cream cheese

1 packet of Bourcin cheese

lemon juice

salt and pepper for seasoning

Mash the avocados into a smooth paste. Mix the Philadelphia cream cheese and the Bourcin in a separate bowl into a smooth cream paste. Add the avocado paste to the cheese paste, add lemon juice, salt and pepper for seasoning. Divide the mixture among individual ramekin dishes and place in the fridge for one hour to firm. Serve with slices of toast.

Carrie's Spinach and Cream Cheese Dip

I used to work in Toronto with Carrie, the owner of this recipe. It is a simple recipe to make and is a fun centrepiece for any party.

First of all, you need a round loaf of bread. Cut out the middle and cube it for dipping.

1 package frozen spinach

1 cup cream cheese

1 cup sour cream

1 can (14 ounces/400 g) water chestnuts, chopped fine

garlic to taste

1 package vegetable or onion soup mix

Defrost the spinach and remove any excess water. Using a blender, cream together the cream cheese, sour cream, water chestnuts, garlic and soup mix for a few seconds. Add the spinach and blend for just one second, then gently place the mixture in the empty bread and assemble the cubes of bread around the base.

Onion and Cheese Tarts

The inspiration behind these next two recipes comes from the fact that I love picnics. These delicious tarts can either be served warm as a starter or cold with a crisp salad at a summer picnic.

The recipe fills 8 prebaked tart cases.

FOR THE PASTRY

6 ounces/170 g plain white flour

2 ounces/50 g butter

1 ounce/30 g lard

1 ounce/30 g grated Parmesan cheese

1 rounded teaspoon dried mixed herbs

FOR THE FILLING

1 ounce/30 g butter

2 large Spanish onions, finely chopped

salt, black pepper and cayenne pepper

6 fl. ounces/180 ml single cream

2 extra large eggs, beaten

$1/2$ teaspoon mustard powder

2 ounces/50 g strong Cheddar cheese, grated

1 ounce/30 g grated Parmesan cheese

Preheat the oven to 350°F/180°C/Gas 4. You'll need two 4-hole (or one 8-hole) patty tins of the kind used for Yorkshire pudding: the holes are 4 inches/10 cm in diameter and $3/4$ inch/2 cm deep. Lightly grease the tins. You'll also need a 5 inch/13 cm cutter.

TO MAKE THE PASTRY

Sift the flour into a bowl and lightly rub in the fats with your fingertips. When the mixture resembles breadcrumbs, add Parmesan and herbs, then sprinkle in enough cold water to bring the dough together and leave the sides of the bowl clean. Place the dough in a polythene bag and leave to rest in the fridge for about 20 minutes.

After that sprinkle some flour on a flat surface and roll the dough out fairly thinly. Use the cutter (or a suitably sized saucer and a sharp knife) to cut out 8 rounds. Fit the pastry rounds into the greased tins, then prick the bases and sides with a fork. Now bake them in the oven for 15–20 minutes or until the pastry is cooked through but only lightly coloured, then remove from the oven but leave them in their tins.

TO MAKE THE FILLING

Melt the butter in a large frying pan, add the onions and toss them around over medium heat to brown at edges. After about 5 minutes, season with salt and both types of peppers, then turn down the heat to low and let them cook slowly for a further 30 minutes. Now divide the onions between the tart cases. In a jug whisk the cream, eggs and mustard powder together, and pour carefully over the onion fillings.

Sprinkle the Cheddar and Parmesan over and bake at 375°F/190°C/Gas 5 for 30 minutes and serve warm.

Tomato and Red Pepper Tarts

Serves 8.

FOR THE PASTRY (SEE PREVIOUS PAGE FOR METHOD)

6 ounces/170 g plain white flour

2 ounces/50 g butter

1 ounce/30 g lard

1 ounce/30 g grated Parmesan cheese

1 rounded teaspoon dried mixed herbs

FOR THE FILLING

2 medium red bell peppers

2 tablespoons olive oil

1 large clove garlic, crushed

one 15 ounce/425 g can and one 8 ounce/ 225 g can Italian chopped tomatoes

2 ounce/50 g can anchovy fillets in oil

$^1/_2$ teaspoon dried thyme

1 dessertspoon tomato purée

salt and freshly milled black pepper

1 egg and 2 egg yolks

1 teaspoon hot paprika

1 small fresh full-fat goat's cheese, rinded

8 sprigs fresh thyme, to garnish

a little extra virgin olive oil to finish

First of all de-seed and chop the bell peppers into small dice. In a large frying pan heat 1 tablespoon olive oil. Add the bell peppers and cook them over medium heat until they're soft and slightly brown at the edges (about 6 minutes). Now stir in the garlic and let that cook for about a minute, then pour in both cans of tomatoes. Pour the anchovies over the tomatoes, then pour in the anchovy oil.

Add the thyme, tomato purée and a seasoning of salt and pepper, then let the mixture simmer gently (without covering) until all the liquid from the tomatoes has evaporated and you have a thick, jam-like consistency. This will take about 20–25 minutes. Remove the sauce to a bowl and leave to cool a little.

Now you need to increase the oven temperature to 375°F/190°C/Gas 5. In a small bowl whisk the egg and egg yolks with the paprika, then stir into the cooled tomato mixture with the other tablespoon of olive oil. Mix everything together, taste to check seasoning, then spoon into tart cases (see previous page).

Finally cut two $^1/_4$ inch/$^1/_2$ cm slices from the round of goat's cheese and cut each into quarters. Lay a quarter in the centre of each tart, press in a sprig of thyme, and bake for 25–30 minutes. Serve warm from the oven with a few drops of olive oil sprinkled over.

Twice-Baked Cheese
Soufflés with Chives

Most people fear the thought of making soufflés but this is undoubtedly my favourite – it has never let me down. Even when served outdoors in a marquee, it always rises to the occasion and tastes delicious.

Serves 4.

8 fl. ounces/240 ml milk

1 small onion, cut in half

1 bay leaf

a little freshly grated nutmeg

salt and freshly milled black pepper

1 ounce/30 g unsalted butter

1 ounce/30 g self-raising flour

2 large eggs, separated

4 ounces/110 g double Gloucester cheese
     with chives

1 teaspoon fresh snipped chives

freshly grated Parmesan cheese

a few sprigs of watercress to garnish

You will require four 5 ounce/150 ml ramekins, well-buttered.

Preheat the oven to 350°F/180°C/Gas 4.

Begin by placing the milk, onion, bay leaf, a good scraping of whole nutmeg and some salt and pepper in a small saucepan. Slowly bring it up to simmering point, then strain it into a jug and discard the onion and bay leaf.

Now rinse and dry the saucepan, place it back on heat and melt the butter in it. Stir in the flour and cook gently for one minute, stirring all the time, to make a smooth, glossy paste. Now add the hot milk mixture little by little, stirring well after each addition. When all the milk is incorporated, let the sauce barely bubble and thicken, then leave it on the lowest possible heat for 2 minutes.

Now take the sauce off the heat and transfer it to a large mixing bowl, then beat in first the egg yolks followed by three-quarters of the grated Gloucester cheese and the snipped chives. Mix everything thoroughly together, and taste to check the seasoning.

Next, the egg whites should go into another bowl and be whisked up to the soft peak stage. Then take a heaped tablespoonful at a time and fold the egg whites into the cheese and egg mixture, using cutting and folding movements so as not to lose the air. Now divide the mixture between the buttered dishes, place them in a roasting tin, and pour in about $1/2$ inch/1 cm of boiling water straight from the kettle.

Place the roasting tin on a high shelf in the oven and bake the soufflés for 10–12 minutes or until they are set and feel springy in the centre (it is important not to undercook them at this stage because on the second cooking they are going to be turned out). Don't worry if they rise up a lot – as they cool they will sink back into the dish. Remove from the roasting tin straight away, then cool and chill in the fridge until needed (they can also be frozen at this stage).

To serve the soufflés, preheat the oven to 400°F/200°C/Gas 6. Butter a solid baking sheet, then slide the point of a small knife round each soufflé, turn it out onto the palm of your hand and place it the right way up on the baking sheet. Keep them well apart. Sprinkle the remaining grated Gloucester cheese on top of each one, then pop them into the oven on the highest shelf and bake for 20–25 minutes or until they're puffy, well-risen and golden brown.

Using a fish slice, slide each one on to a hot serving plate and serve straight away with some freshly grated Parmesan sprinkled over and a few sprigs of watercress as a garnish.

NOTE: If you wish, cook the soufflés a second time in the dishes without turning them out. If you're freezing them, make quite sure they are thoroughly defrosted before cooking.

Twice-Baked Cheese Soufflé with Chives

Patsy Crosse's Avocado and Tomato Terrine

Patsy Crosse's Avocado and Tomato Terrine

This recipe was given to me by Patsy Crosse whom I got to know in Bahrain. Lovingly known as "The Duchess", she is definitely one of the best cooks I have ever known. She was truly talented in the kitchen and took great pride in everything she cooked. Sadly, she passed away in 2000 and we miss her wonderful food. This recipe of hers is one of my favourites and is best served as an entrée with a good glass of white wine.

AVOCADO TERRINE

6 medium avocados

3 tablespoons lemon juice

1/4 pint/120 ml dry white wine

1/2 pint/240 ml chicken stock

3 sachets gelatine

1 large clove garlic, chopped

dash of Tabasco sauce

1 tablespoon Lea & Perrins Worcestershire sauce

salt and pepper

1/2 pint/240 ml double whipped cream (or substitute mayonnaise)

VINAIGRETTE (MIX ALL TOGETHER)

2 teaspoons sugar

1/4 teaspoon salt

1/2 teaspoon mustard

2 tablespoons cider vinegar

5 tablespoons olive oil

2 tomatoes, chopped into small cubes

3 spring onions, chopped finely

lots of basil, chopped finely

Line a 9 inch/23 cm loaf tin with cling film, pressing it carefully into the corners. Cut each avocado in half and carefully remove the skin from the back of the 3 most perfect halves and brush them with lemon juice. Cut the tops of the 3 halves and set aside with the unpeeled halves.

Scoop out the flesh of the avocados and reserve. Put the white wine and stock in a saucepan, sprinkle with the gelatine and heat until it dissolves. Add this to the avocado flesh in a food processor and blend to purée. Then add garlic, Tabasco, Worcestershire sauce, salt and pepper and whipped cream and blend again.

Pour half the purée into the loaf tin. Arrange the 3 avocado halves in the centre, round side down, then pour in the rest of the purée. Cover with cling film and refrigerate for 3–4 hours.

Carefully remove the terrine from the tin by turning it upside down and gently removing the cling film.

Put all the vinaigrette ingredients into a blender and mix for 2 minutes. Serve the avocado terrine in slices and pour small quantities of the vinaigrette over each slice.

Trisha Chapman's Zucchini Slices

I first tasted this recipe on Big Wave Bay beach in Hong Kong with Iain (my boyfriend at the time) and his parents. Trisha, renowned for being an excellent cook, kindly passed this recipe on to me several years ago. It remains one of my favourite picnic recipes.

Serves 4–6.

13 1/2 ounces/380 g zucchini

1 large onion

3 rashers bacon (optional)

1 cup grated Cheddar cheese

1 cup self-raising flour, sifted

1/2 cup oil

5 eggs

salt and pepper

a sprinkle of fresh rosemary

Grate the zucchini coarsely, and finely chop the onion and bacon. Combine the zucchini, onion, bacon, cheese, sifted flour, oil and lightly beaten eggs, then season with salt and pepper. Pour into a well-oiled tin or dish measuring 6 inches x 10 inches/15 cm x 25 cm and bake in a moderate oven 30–40 minutes or until brown. Serve with a sprinkle of fresh rosemary.

I halved this very satisfactorily using 3 eggs and actually less than half the flour and oil.

Tarte au Beaufort

This recipe comes from the owners of a delightful restaurant in Val d'Isère, France, and can be described as something between a tart, a quiche and a soufflé, the result being a fabulous combination of richness and taste. It is very important to buy the correct Beaufort cheese, otherwise it will turn out as an unattractive sunken soufflé. I have fond memories of this dish. Several years ago in Hong Kong, my boyfriend at the time, Tom, invited his stepfather Marty over for lunch. As it was a hot day I thought a light salad with this Tarte would be a fine combination. Unfortunately Marty, who is usually on time, turned up an hour late and it was a very disappointing and embarrassing lunch as the soufflé sank along with my ego!

Serves 8.

THE PASTRY

5 ounces/140 g butter

10 ounces/280 g flour

a pinch of salt

1 egg

a little water

THE FILLING

1 pound/450 g Beaufort cheese

4 eggs

1 soupspoon flour

2 soupspoons milk

17 fl. ounces/$1/2$ litre cream

a pinch of mustard

a pinch of salt

ground pepper

OTHER MATERIALS

tart mould or baking tin,
    11 inches/28 cm in diameter

Take the butter out of the fridge, and cut into small pieces. Put the flour and salt into a salad bowl, make a hole, and break the egg into it. Mix the flour and egg, then the pieces of butter, with fingertips. Add the water bit by bit to obtain a firm paste. Mould it into a ball, wrap in cling film and leave it in the fridge for 30 minutes.

At the end of this time, roll out the dough, covering the pre-buttered mould. Poke some holes in the bottom with a fork, and put it in the oven for 10 minutes.

Grate the cheese.

Separate the whites and yolks of the eggs. Put the yolks into a bowl and mix with the flour, milk, cream and cheese, and add mustard, salt and pepper. Beat the whites until stiff and fold it gently into the mixture. Pour it into the semi-cooked pastry.

Cook in the oven (300°F/150°C/Gas 2), for 30 minutes.

Serve immediately with a green crunchy salad.

Georgia Brown's Roasted Red Peppers and Tomatoes

Try to find large, juicy, sweet bell peppers for this recipe. Kindly donated by Georgia Brown, mother of my godson, this makes an excellent starter for a dinner party.

Serves 2.

1 red bell pepper

1 tomato

capers

anchovies

2 fresh olives

garlic (optional)

salt and pepper

olive oil

Cut the red bell pepper in half. Leave the stalk on, but take out the pips. Cut the tomato in half, and place it on the red bell pepper. Crush capers, anchovies, olives (plus optional garlic) and salt and pepper together and place on top of the tomato. Put a fresh olive on top.

Place in a 400°F/200°C/Gas 6 oven and cook for an hour. Brush with lots of olive oil before cooking.

Sometimes I add just a dash of sugar and balsamic vinegar for a perfect taste.

Garlic Chives and Blue Cheese Soufflé

This can be made in either small ramekin dishes as a starter or served in one large ramekin as an extra vegetable dish. This is rather rich but makes a great presentation at the table.

Serves 8–10.

1 tablespoon butter

1 tablespoon olive oil

4 cloves garlic, peeled and crushed

2 cups milk

3/4 cup flour, sifted

salt and pepper

3 1/2 ounces/100 g blue cheese, e.g. Kikorangi

1/4 cup grated Cheddar

1 bunch garlic chives (2 tablespoons, chopped)

8 eggs, separated

Preheat the oven to 375°F/190°C/Gas 5. Grease 8–10 small ramekins. Heat the butter and oil in a large saucepan and sauté the garlic until it is soft. Add the milk and bring to the boil. Remove from the heat and soak for 5 minutes. Return to the boil and whisk in the flour gently. Be careful it doesn't become lumpy. Cook for 3–4 minutes at a gentle simmer, then season well and allow to cool.

Add the cheeses, chives and yolks, beating them in with a wooden spoon. Whisk the egg whites to soft peaks and fold gently into the mixture. Pour into ramekin dishes and bake about 20 minutes or until the soufflés are puffed and golden. Serve immediately.

Cape Lodge Bircher Muesli

I have three recipes for Bircher Muesli and all of them are different depending on how health-conscious you are. The Cape Lodge muesli I discovered while staying in Perth with a great friend Deborah Morgan. It is a light muesli served with milk. The Huka Lodge muesli is my favourite since it is rich, thick and has a lot of cream. Huka Lodge is one of my favourite hotels in the world and is situated on the shores of Lake Taupo in New Zealand. The third muesli I have had for many years and is a perfect combination of the other two recipes.

rolled oats

nuts (almonds and brazil nuts), oven-roasted

honey

sugar

dried fruits – apricots, chopped, and sultanas

toasted coconut

milk

orange juice (a small amount)

NOTE: Quantities of ingredients are to taste. Mix all the ingredients together and add the milk to just below the level of the mixture. Top up with orange juice till just covered. Place in the fridge overnight until milk is absorbed, and stir well.

Paris

Huka Lodge Bircher Muesli

BASE RECIPE

1 1/2 pounds/680 g rolled oats

9 ounces/250 g ground hazelnuts

12 1/2 ounces/350 g sugar

3 1/3 pounds/1 1/2 kg apples, peeled and grated

4 cups orange juice

7 ounces/200 g sultanas

2 ounces/50 g honey

Mix all the ingredients together and refrigerate for 12 hours.

1 1/3 pounds/600 g fresh fruit

7 fl. ounces/210 ml whipped cream

10 ounces/280 g natural yoghurt

Mix all these ingredients together with 2 1/4 pounds/1 kg of the base recipe as required. Serve cold at breakfast.

Bircher Muesli

2 ounces/50 g white oats

2 ounces/50 g rolled oats

cold milk

1/3 ounce/10 g grated carrots

1/3 ounce/10 g grated apple

a bit of almond flakes

a bit of pistachios

2 ounces/50 g yoghurt

honey to taste

orange segments

Soak the oats in cold milk for 1 hour. Mix them with all the other ingredients. Garnish with orange segments.

Salad of Cucumber, White Radish, Pumpkin Seeds and Roasted Apples in Lime Vinaigrette

Salad of Cucumber, White Radish, Pumpkin Seeds and Roasted Apples in Lime Vinaigrette

I recently discovered this sensational salad staying at the King Pacific Lodge, a fishing lodge on Princess Royal Island in British Columbia. I contemplated putting this recipe under the Salad section but it is really a starter or an individual course rather than a large salad in a bowl. It is incredibly light and the wonderful combination of vegetables, pumpkin seeds and roasted apples creates a fresh, light starter.

Serves 4.

SALAD

2 Granny Smith apples

1 tablespoon olive oil

1 English cucumber, julienned

1 radish, julienned

1/4 cup toasted pumpkin seeds

VINAIGRETTE

3 limes

2 tablespoons honey

1/2 cup grapeseed oil (vary according to acidity of limes)

salt and pepper

For the salad, first cut the apples in half, core, then roast at 375°F/190°C/Gas 5 for 10 minutes in olive oil. Cool.

To make the vinaigrette, mix the juice of 3 limes with honey and grapeseed oil. Season with salt and pepper.

Toss the julienned salad with the lime vinaigrette and allow to absorb.

Place the mixed salad over the roasted apple with toasted pumpkin seeds, then pour over the remaining lime vinaigrette.

Jane Normanton's Katharine Wheels with Roasted Peppers and Asparagus

This recipe was given to me by Jane Normanton, my stepmother Lyn's best friend. Jane is an excellent vegetarian cook and this recipe is just one of her own exquisite creations.

Serves 4 or 5.

1 sheet puff pastry, rolled thinly

6 asparagus spears, just cooked

1 packet (4 ounces/110 g) Feta cheese, grated

4 red bell peppers, roasted and skinned

1 tablespoon chopped chives

1 ounce/30 g pine kernels

1/2 mild red chilli, finely chopped

1 egg, beaten, to glaze

TOMATO SAUCE (BLEND TOGETHER)

1 onion

1 can (14 ounces/400 g) tomatoes

1 green or red bell pepper

salt and pepper

Roll out the pastry thinly to about 12 inches/30 cm square. First put a line of asparagus along one edge, then a 1 inch/2 1/2 cm line of grated Feta cheese, followed by a line of roasted red bell pepper strips, another line of Feta, then another line of bell peppers. Sprinkle with chopped chives, pine kernels and chilli. Brush the pastry edges with a bit of beaten egg.

Now roll up the pastry into a tight long roll. Cut into 1 inch/2 1/2 cm circles. Place these circles on a baking tray and brush the tops with the remaining egg mixture. Bake in a hot oven for 15–20 minutes. Serve with a simple tomato sauce.

TO GRILL/ROAST PEPPERS

Heat the grill. Set the whole bell pepper on the rack about 4 inches/10 cm from heat and grill, turning as needed, until the skin is black and blistered, about 10–12 minutes. Immediately put the bell pepper in a plastic bag, close it and leave until it is cool enough to handle. (The steam trapped in the bag helps loosen the skin.) With a table knife, peel off the skin. Cut around the core and pull it out. Halve the bell pepper and scrape away the seeds. Rinse the bell pepper under running water and pat dry. Cut each bell pepper into strips.

Lobster and Lime Tartar on Avocado Carpaccio

Lobster and Lime Tartar on Avocado Carpaccio

This recipe comes from Phillip, the charming head chef at one of Hong Kong's top hotels. The occasion was a farewell party when I was saying goodbye to some of my closest friends. I decided to book 12 of us in for cookery lessons, followed by lunch consisting of our own creations. The result was this very elegant starter which only one of my guests, Callie Botsford, was able to replicate!

Makes 10 portions.

1 1/2 pounds/680 g Boston lobster meat

salt and cayenne pepper

2 ounces/50 g vine tomatoes

14 ounces/400 g avocado (about 3 ounces/80 g meat)

1 lime for zest and juice

7 ounces/200 g sour cream

pepper

2 1/2 ounces/85 g mixed salad

2 fl. ounces/60 ml olive oil

1 fl. ounce/30 ml balsamic vinegar

Hong Kong Harbour

Cook the lobster in boiling water with plenty of salt and cayenne pepper for 1 minute and then allow to cool on a tray.

Blanch the tomatoes in the same water for about 8 seconds and refresh in ice water. Peel and de-seed the tomatoes and cut into dice.

Mash the avocado with a fork and mix with a little salt and half the lime juice to a purée. Divide 1 ounce/30 g each into 4 small vacuum bags. Spread very thinly and evenly and freeze until very hard. (You can prepare this the day before.)

When the lobster is still slightly warm, break out the meat and discard any excess water. Chop into a very fine mass and mix with sour cream, lime zest, lime juice, a little salt and pepper and finally the fresh tomatoes.

Mix the salad with olive oil and balsamic vinegar. Transfer the frozen avocado carefully onto four plates and defrost. Place the salad in the middle and then two quenelles of lobster tartar left and right of the salad. Serve with some white baguette bread if you wish.

Tomato Tarte Tatin with Goat Cheese

This dish comes from the south of France and is a fabulous opportunity to use up all those late-season tomatoes.

Serves 8.

1 sheet prepared butter puff pastry, cut to fit a 10 inch/25 cm cooking pan

4 tablespoons sugar

4 tablespoons sherry or cider vinegar

4 tablespoons water

2 ounces/50 g butter

salt and pepper

6 ripe Roma tomatoes, peeled and halved lengthwise

freshly shaved mature goat cheese

Chill the pastry in the refrigerator until ready to use. Preheat the oven to 425°F/220°C/Gas 7.

Place a wide, heavy-based 10 inch/25 cm ovenproof frying pan over high heat and sprinkle over the sugar, shaking the pan to distribute and cook it evenly. As the sugar starts to caramelise, continue shaking and tipping the pan to help it cook evenly. When the sugar is quite dark but not burnt, hold the pan away from you and add the vinegar (it will spit and sputter). Add the water and return the pan to low heat until the caramel has dissolved. Stir in the butter, season to taste, then place the tomatoes, cut side up, evenly around the pan. Roast in the oven for 10 minutes or until softened but not soggy. The caramel should be thick. If it is not, return it to the stove top and boil until thickened.

Remove the pastry from the refrigerator and carefully drape it over the tomatoes, taking care that the pastry is tucked down inside the edges of the pan. Bake for about 10–15 minutes or until the pastry is a dark golden colour on top. Remove from the oven and allow to sit for 5 minutes before inverting onto a plate. If the tart is left any longer than 5 minutes the caramel may set firmly and need reheating to be removed. Set aside to cool to room temperature, then serve topped with the shaved goat cheese.

Tomato Tarte Tatin with Goat Cheese

Eggplant and Goat Cheese Sandwiches with Tomato Vinaigrette

This has to be one of my favourite and most-used recipes: simple, delicious, and the presentation is so eye-catching it leaves guests asking for the recipe. It is also a good standby substitute dish at dinner parties when you need to have a vegetarian variety as an added item to suit everyone's needs.

2 medium eggplants

oil for deep-frying

2 large red bell peppers

14 ounce/400 g piece goat cheese

PESTO

2 cups firmly packed fresh basil leaves

$1/2$ cup olive oil

1 clove garlic, crushed

$2/3$ cup grated Parmesan cheese

TOMATO VINAIGRETTE

2 medium egg tomatoes, chopped

$2/3$ cup olive oil

2 tablespoons white vinegar

$1/2$ teaspoon sugar

Cut each eggplant into 10 slices about $1/2$ inch/1 cm thick. Deep-fry the eggplants in hot oil until browned, then drain on absorbent paper and cool.

Quarter the peppers and remove the seeds and membranes. Grill the bell peppers, skin side up, until the skin blisters and blackens. Peel away the skin, cut the peppers into 1 inch/$2^1/2$ cm strips, and cool.

With a hot knife, cut the cheese into 10 slices about $1/3$ inch/$8^1/2$ mm thick.

Just before serving, place an eggplant slice on a serving plate, top with a slice of cheese, 2 strips of pepper, pesto, another slice of eggplant and more pesto. Spoon the tomato vinaigrette onto the plate. Repeat with the remaining ingredients.

PESTO

Blend the basil, oil and garlic until smooth. Stir in the cheese.

TOMATO VINAIGRETTE

Blend the tomatoes until smooth, and push through a sieve, discarding the pulp. Combine the tomato purée with the remaining ingredients in a jar and shake well.

Roast Red Pepper Soufflé

This great-tasting soufflé is easy to make, yet looks impressive at any dinner party, served either in one large dish or in small individual ramekin dishes. This must be served immediately after cooking, as like all soufflés it will begin to sink when taken out of the oven.

FOR THE ONION MARMALADE

1½ pounds/680 g red onions

1½ ounces/40 g unsalted butter

3 ounces/85 g demerara sugar

1½ tablespoons crème de cassis

2½ tablespoons sherry vinegar

2 teaspoons salt

FOR THE RED PEPPER SOUFFLÉ

2 ounces/50 g unsalted butter, plus extra for greasing

1½ ounces/40 g plain flour

½ cup milk

slice of onion or ½ shallot

10 ounces/280 g red bell peppers, roasted, skinned and seeded (see page 39)

1 teaspoon tomato juice

1 teaspoon lemon juice

white pepper

2 ounces/50 g Parmesan cheese

2 free-range egg yolks

3 egg whites at room temperature

sea salt

cream of tartar (optional)

FOR THE ONION MARMALADE

Peel and finely slice the onions, melt the butter in a heavy-bottomed pan and sweat the onions gently until softened but not coloured. Add the other ingredients and cook uncovered on low heat, stirring occasionally for about 90 minutes, until the mixture becomes a moist and soft marmalade. Cool and reserve.

FOR THE RED PEPPER SOUFFLÉ

Butter and chill 4 ramekins. Melt more butter in a heavy-bottomed pan, then gently cook the flour until there is a nutty smell. Set aside.

Warm the milk gently with onion or shallot and allow to infuse for 15 minutes off the heat. Chop the roasted bell peppers (see page 39) roughly, then purée in a food processor, adding tomato juice and lemon juice. Warm the butter and flour mixture then remove from heat and add strained milk, then pepper purée, stirring constantly. Add a little white pepper to taste, if required.

Cook over low heat, stirring regularly for about 40 minutes, when the texture should be noticeably lighter.

Place the grated Parmesan in a heatproof glass bowl and add the pepper mixture; fold together until the cheese is amalgamated. Cool. Beat the egg yolks and add to the pepper mixture.

Beat the egg whites until frothy, then add a pinch of salt and a pinch of cream of tartar. Continue to beat until firm peaks form.

Blend the egg white with a whisk into pepper mix, then fold in the remainder with a spatula. Fill up the ramekins, smoothing the tops with a palette knife. Loosen the mixture from the side of the ramekin with the point of a knife.

Cook for 25 minutes in a roasting tray filled with boiling water to two-thirds of the way up in an oven preheated to 375°F/190°C/Gas 5. Soufflés should be well risen and slightly browned.

Serve immediately with a spoonful of tepid marmalade alongside. Any marmalade remaining will keep in the refrigerator for about 2 weeks, as long as it is in a sealed jar.

Italian Chicken Livers on Bruchetta

I learnt to cook these next two recipes whilst attending Italian cooking classes in a divine little village called Il Borro in Tuscany. The scrumptious bruchettas are simple to make and are perfectly complemented by a glass of white wine at the end of a sunny day. For the Vitello Tonnato I suggest serving only small portions for either a starter or a light lunch as it is very rich!

RATOUILLE

1 onion

2 cloves garlic

2 carrots

2 stalks celery

pinch of sugar

salt and pepper

olive oil

1 can (14 ounces/400 g) tomatoes

1 sprig basil

2 teaspoons tomato purée

CHICKEN LIVERS

olive oil

1 red onion, chopped

4 cloves garlic

1 stalk celery (including leaves), chopped

3¹/₂ ounces/100 g capers

2 anchovies, chopped

2¹/₄ pounds/1 kg chicken livers, roughly chopped

¹/₂ cup sweet wine

salt

2 ounces/50 g lard

RATOUILLE

Fry the onion, garlic, carrots, celery, sugar, salt and pepper with the olive oil. Add the can of tomatoes, basil and tomato purée. Cook for 15–20 minutes and cool. Purée the ingredients.

CHICKEN LIVERS

In a large frying pan heat the olive oil and fry all the chicken liver ingredients except wine, salt and lard for 20 minutes or more. Add 2–3 tablespoons of the sweet wine and 3 tablespoons ratouille mixture and salt to taste. Cook further if necessary.

Put the mixture through a liquidiser and return to the pan. Add a little lard and more sweet wine, and water if needed.

Vitello Tonnato

MAYONNAISE

9 egg yolks and 2 egg whites (not whisked separately) at room temperature

4 cups oil (half sunflower oil and half olive oil)

salt

¹/₂ cup capers, chopped finely

juice of 2 lemons

1 tin (7 ounces/200 g) tuna in oil (not water)

pinch of salt

VEAL

1 onion, sliced

1 tomato, quartered

1 carrot, sliced

1 stalk celery or a few sprigs parsley

1¹/₂ pounds/700 g veal

MAYONNAISE

Mix the eggs in a liquidiser, then slowly add oil until thick and creamy. Add salt. Squeeze the juice from the capers and add to the mixture. Add lemon juice and tuna with seasoning. Blend thoroughly and place in the fridge.

VEAL

Put the onion, tomato, carrot, celery (or parsley) and veal into a saucepan of water, enough to cover the ingredients. Bring to the boil and boil for 1–1¹/₂ hours. When cooked, slice veal very thinly. Pour the mayonnaise thinly over veal before serving.

Venice and Sienna

Didi Wills' Salmon Mousse

Didi believes she is famous for her mushroom risotto but I have to disagree – her Salmon Mousse which I first tasted in Singapore several years ago is delicious. This mousse makes a lovely light lunch or even a starter at any casual dinner party.

1 packet salmon

salt and pepper

juice from 1¹/₂ lemons

2 tablespoons cognac

5 fl. ounces/150 ml melted butter

1 cup double cream (whipped)

5 slices of lemon

Chop the salmon in a food processor and add the salt, pepper, and lemon juice. Add the cognac and half the melted butter. Fold the salmon into the cream gently. Place lemon slices on top of the salmon and add the remaining butter through a muslin cloth. Refrigerate for an hour. Serve with slices of toast.

Mrs Wigmore's Smoked Mackerel Pâté

Mrs Wigmore is the reason I am here today. Having been my cooking teacher since I was 11 years old, she has taught me practically everything I know. While this recipe is by no means her best or most complex dish, it is one which is well tested and which I use frequently. This is an easy recipe and tastes great served on toast.

1 fillet smoked mackerel

4 ounces/110 g sieved cottage cheese

4 ounces/110 g softened butter

1 teaspoon horseradish sauce

lemon juice to taste

2–3 tablespoons sour cream

a little grated nutmeg

freshly ground pepper

1 teaspoon sherry

Skin the mackerel and remove the bones. Flake the fish, break it up and blend with the other ingredients until mashed (but as little as possible). Put into ramekin dishes and chill before serving. Serve with slices of toast.

Tomato and Caramelised Onion Flan

Another summer or picnic dish – easy to cook and even easier to eat. Do make sure you find sweet, ripe tomatoes!

Serves 10.

1 tablespoon extra virgin olive oil, plus more for garnishing

8 onions, peeled and roughly sliced

8¹/₂ inch/20 cm short pastry tart shell, baked blind

4 ounces/110 g Gruyère cheese, grated

5–6 vine-ripened tomatoes

1 tablespoon capers, preferably salted

2 tablespoons finely shredded basil

Heat the oil in a large, heavy-based frying pan. Add the onions and stir for 1 minute to coat thoroughly with oil. Turn the heat to the lowest setting and cook for 1–2 hours, stirring occasionally, until the onions are a rich golden brown.

Preheat the oven to 350°F/180°C/Gas 4. Spoon the onions into tart shells, and sprinkle over the Gruyère. Slice the tomatoes crosswise into four pieces and arrange on top. Scatter over the capers (soaked first if necessary) and basil. Drizzle with olive oil, then bake for 20 minutes. Serve warm.

SOUPS

India

Dubai

DUBAI, TIMELESS CITY

Nestling in the golden sand dunes of Arabia on the southern coast of the Gulf, Dubai emerges today as one of the best serviced destinations for tourists in the Gulf region. Once merely a stopover for travellers, this dynamic member of the United Arab Emirates sees an annual growth of visitors filling its luxury hotels and giant shopping malls. Being on the coast, Dubai also offers golden beaches and a royal lifestyle for those who simply want to laze around and leave the shopping to others. There is sporting action, from year-round falconry and camel safaris to the seasonal Dubai World Cup for horse racing enthusiasts and the Dubai Desert Classic for serious golfers.

Dubai's skyline constantly changes in step with its new developments. To go back in time, we went to its ancient quarter, where life revolves around the Creek, a natural inlet that runs through the centre of the city. Just as it has for hundreds of years, the Creek bustles with entrepôt activity – dhows loading and unloading, ferries crossing from side to side, filled with merchants and traders.

Since the dawn of civilisation, the Gulf has been one of the major trade routes of the world, witnessing the movement of silks, carpets and aromatic spices from India and the Orient, frankincense from Oman and pearls from Bahrain and Basra. Goods offloaded from ships were transferred to camel caravans for the overland trek across the Arabian peninsula to the ports of the Mediterranean. Not surprisingly, before the British arrived in the nineteenth century to impose law and order, the Gulf was also a rich hunting ground for pirates and smugglers.

The old quarter still resonates with life. As their counterparts did countless generations ago, the seaport eating houses offer fresh seafood redolent with Middle Eastern spices, eaten with rice and washed down with cardamom coffee or sweet black tea served in tiny glasses or cups.

Dubai has been remarkably successful in grafting a modern infrastructure onto a rich, authentic and colourful past. Besides, having spent all my childhood holidays in Bahrain while growing up – my mother still lives there today, even after 25 years – I feel very comfortable in the Middle East.

Chilled Beetroot Gazpacho

I have many friends who dislike beetroot but I can guarantee that this soup will be loved by all. The strong taste of gazpacho is evident and is delicious when served cold with sprinkles of coriander on top.

1$^1/_2$ pounds/680 g cooked beetroot

$^1/_2$–1 red chilli, seeded, roughly chopped

2 nectarines, peeled, stoned, roughly chopped

$^3/_4$ cucumber, peeled, seeded, roughly chopped

6 large sprigs coriander

10 fl. ounces/300 ml mixed vegetable juice (bottled or in a carton)

2$^1/_2$ fl. ounces/75 ml olive oil

1–2 tablespoons lemon juice

salt and freshly ground black pepper

FOR THE GARNISH

$^1/_4$ cucumber, peeled and seeded

$^1/_2$ small shallot, finely diced

1 tablespoon freshly chopped coriander

pinch of sugar

salt, freshly ground black pepper

lemon juice to taste

ice cubes, whole or crushed (optional)

Chilled Beetroot Gazpacho

Peel the beetroot if necessary. Roughly chop and put into a food processor or liquidiser, then process into very small chunks.

Add the chilli, nectarine, cucumber, coriander and half the vegetable juice. Process to a smooth paste. Gradually add the olive oil and remaining vegetable juice. Taste, season with lemon juice, salt and pepper. Refrigerate until very cold.

To prepare the garnish, finely dice the cucumber, then mix with the shallot and coriander. Season with a pinch of sugar, salt and pepper. Stir in lemon juice to taste. Refrigerate for at least half an hour for the flavours to develop.

Before serving, re-taste the gazpacho when it is very cold and add seasoning if necessary. Pour into six individual soup bowls. If using crushed ice, stir it into the garnish and spoon on top of the soup, in the centre of each bowl. Alternatively, add a whole ice cube to the soup and sprinkle with the garnish.

Samantha Pooley's Pumpkin and Bacon Soup

My gorgeous sister has become something of a wonderful cook in the last few years and this pumpkin and bacon soup is just one of her delicious recipes. This winter soup looks beautiful presented and served in tiny pumpkins with scatterings of pumpkin seeds. This is perfect for a winter meal or Thanksgiving.

Serves 8.

8 mini pumpkins or 1 medium-sized pumpkin

3 tablespoons vegetable oil plus more for deep-frying

salt

8 rashers of smoked bacon, chopped

1 tablespoon cumin powder

1 tablespoon coriander powder

1 cup onion, sliced thin

3 tablespoons unsalted butter

4–5 cups chicken stock

pepper

Preheat oven to 275°F/140°C/Gas 1.

Cut the top quarter off the pumpkins, reserving the lids. Scrape out the pumpkin seeds, clean and rinse, then pat dry. Toss with 3 tablespoons of oil, add salt to taste, then arrange in one layer on a baking sheet. Bake in the middle of the oven, stirring occasionally for 1 to 1¼ hours or until golden and crisp.

In a separate pan, fry the chopped bacon and add the cumin and coriander. Fry until crispy but not burnt.

Increase the oven heat to 350°F/180°C/Gas 4. Bake the pumpkins and lids (cut side down) on lightly-oiled baking sheets until tender. This will take roughly 30–40 minutes. Scrape out most of the pulp, but leave just enough for the pumpkins to retain their shape. Reserve all the pulp.

Cook the onion in the butter in a skillet over low heat for 5 minutes or until it is softened. Add the pumpkin pulp, chicken stock and bacon. Simmer for 20 minutes. Purée the mixture in batches using a blender and transfer to a saucepan. Add chicken stock to thin if necessary.

TO SERVE

Warm the pumpkin shells and lids in a 350°F/180°C/Gas 4 oven for 15 minutes. Heat the soup, adding broth to thin slightly if necessary. Add salt and pepper to taste. Put the pumpkin shells into shallow soup bowls and ladle soup into each shell. Top with the toasted pumpkin seeds. Put the lid on, slightly askew.

Kate Sasson's Apple, Carrot and Coriander Soup

I only discovered this recipe recently when having dinner at the house of my dear friend Didi Wills. In fact this recipe originated from a mutual friend called Kate Sasson, who is a fabulous creative cook. Remember to serve this cold: you will be amazed at the exquisite refreshing taste and texture of this soup.

1 onion, chopped

1 tablespoon butter

2 carrots, coarsely chopped

4 Granny Smith apples, coarsely chopped

$1/2$ cup coriander, coarsely chopped

4 cups vegetable stock

salt to taste

1 teaspoon freshly ground pepper

Zucchini Almond Soup

Sauté the onion with butter, then add the chopped carrots. Stir for 5 minutes. Add the chopped apples and the coriander, stir for 1 minute, then pour in the vegetable stock. Simmer for 15 minutes or until the vegetables are cooked. Season with salt and pepper. Cool, then purée.

Refrigerate until needed. Serve cold and garnish with coarsely chopped fresh coriander.

Zucchini Almond Soup

While staying in a fabulous log cabin called Kachemak Bay in Alaska, we were served with wonderful, wholesome home-cooked food. This soup is just one of their recipes.

olive oil

3 cloves garlic, diced

8–10 medium zucchini, peeled and chopped

1 medium yellow onion, diced

$2/3$ cup almonds, sliced and toasted

sage or basil (optional)

3 tablespoons or more Amaretto liqueur

milk

salt and pepper to taste

Heat the oil and sauté all the above ingredients except liqueur and milk for at least 30 minutes.

Add the Amaretto and blend everything, cup by cup, in a blender with milk until correct consistency is reached. Add salt and pepper to taste. Serve hot.

Truffled Pea Soup with Mint and Parmesan

This is another of my favourite soups and it comes from Huka Lodge in New Zealand. Serve this only in small quantities as it is rather rich. It makes a wonderful starter in winter. Best to use fresh peas or *petit pois* to extract the real taste from the peas.

Serves 6.

1 pound/450 g freshly shelled peas

7 fl. ounces/210 ml chicken stock

3 ounces/85 g unsalted butter

cream

1 fl. ounce/30 ml truffle oil

6 teaspoons finely grated Parmesan

3 teaspoons finely shredded mint

6 tablespoons small croutons, fried in bacon
    fat and a little butter until golden brown

milk

Cook the peas in the stock with butter until stock is reduced and butter forms a glaze coating the peas. Blend well to a fine purée. Return to a clean pot and add cream until the desired consistency is reached. Boil and strain through a fine sieve, pushing hard on solids. Keep warm.

Divide garnishes (truffle oil, Parmesan, mint and croutons) evenly and swirl in a little milk to mix.

Truffled Pea Soup with Mint and Parmesan

Essence of Tomato with Baked Tomato and Basil

Serves 6.

7 pounds/3 kg ripe vine tomatoes
    (Roma or San Marzano)

1/2 stalk celery, chopped

4 ounces/110 g basil leaves

FOR 2 LITRES OF ESSENCE, ADD

pinch of salt

a bit of Lea & Perrins
    Worcestershire sauce

a bit of Tabasco sauce

TO SERVE

3 ripe tomatoes, peeled and seeded

6 basil leaves

salt and pepper

Place the tomatoes, celery and basil leaves into a robo-coupe and process. Pour the mixture into a stainless steel pot and simmer gently for 15 minutes. Strain through a coffee filter or hang in a cheesecloth to drain. Season with salt, Worcestershire and Tabasco sauces.

TO SERVE

Quarter the tomatoes and sandwich basil leaves between every two quarters. Season with salt and pepper and bake at 350°F/180°C/Gas 4 for ten minutes. Place each into a soup plate and carefully pour the essence over it.

NOTE: An extravagant amount of good, ripe tomatoes is needed to produce a fairly small amount of essence, which has to be absolutely clear.

Corn Soup

Corn is one of my favourite vegetables. I discovered this soup with Rob whilst passing by a quaint little café in a town near Berkeley, USA. It is light and not too thick in substance but incredibly tasty and succulent served with hot crusty rolls.

8 tablespoons butter

4 onions, diced

4 quarts/4 1/2 litres water

20 ears of corn, kernels cut from cob or 1
    packet frozen corn

salt and pepper

Melt the butter, and add onions and 1 cup of water. Cover and simmer for 10 minutes. Add the remaining water and bring to the boil. Add the corn and bring to the boil, then simmer for 5 minutes.

Purée and strain. Add salt and pepper to taste. Serve piping hot with a fresh crusty roll.

Daisy Paciente's Broccoli and Stilton Soup

Daisy has worked for me now for over 7 years and when she first arrived at the house she struggled to cook a boiled egg. Today she is a remarkable chef, trying out different recipes and cooking for dinner parties without hesitation. This wonderfully warming soup is just a taste of her accomplished culinary skills.

2 broccoli florets

2 tablespoons butter

1 onion, chopped

1 leek, white part only, chopped

1 small potato, diced

1 stalk celery, chopped

3 cups chicken stock

1 cup milk

2 tablespoons cream

salt and pepper

5 ounces/140 g Stilton cheese
    (blue Stilton), crumbled

Chop the broccoli, discarding the tough stems.

Melt the butter in a saucepan and cook the onion and leek for 3 minutes. Add the broccoli, potato and celery, stir, then pour in the stock. Cover and simmer for 20 minutes.

Cool, then purée in a blender.

Add the milk, cream and seasoning, then reheat in a saucepan. Add the crumbled cheese until it just melts.

Before serving, add salt and pepper to taste. Serve with blanched broccoli florets on top.

Broccoli Cauliflower Soup

Serves 4.

1 pound/450 g broccoli

1/2 pound/225 g cauliflower

1 medium onion, chopped

1 clove garlic, crushed

2 cups water

1 small chicken stock cube, crumbled

1 medium potato, chopped

2 small stalks celery, chopped

1/2 teaspoon dried marjoram leaves

1 cup skimmed milk

1 tablespoon chopped fresh parsley

Cut the broccoli and cauliflower into flowerets.

Combine the onion and garlic in a large saucepan with 1 tablespoon of the water, stirring constantly over heat until onion is soft (or microwave on High for about 5 minutes). Add the remaining water, stock cube, potato, celery, broccoli and cauliflower. Bring to the boil, reduce heat, simmer for 10 minutes or until potato is tender (or microwave on high heat for about 10 minutes). Add the marjoram.

Blend or process the broccoli mixture until smooth. Return to the pan, add milk and parsley, and reheat just before serving.

Clarke Quay, Singapore

Anne Bosomworth's Vegetable Soup

While the instructions of this easy-to-make soup are to fry and simmer, I was shown how to make it in five minutes in a microwave oven. I used to eat this soup every day when staying at Glenhead Farm in Scotland, one of my favourite places in the world.

4 carrots

1 potato

2 stalks celery

1 leek

1 large onion

butter

2 cups chicken stock

1 chicken and ham Knorr's packet soup

Chop all the vegetables finely and sauté them in a frying pan with the butter. Leave for approximately 10–15 minutes. Add the chicken stock and the soup mixture and cook for a further 25 minutes. Remove and blend for 2–3 minutes. It is important not to overblend but to leave some of the vegetables still visible so as to make a hearty homemade soup.

For quick lunches, it is easy just to put all the ingredients into the microwave for 10 minutes. The result is very similar.

White Bean Soup

This is an unusual soup in the sense that it looks like a hot tomato soup, but this soup is served cold and the combination of the white beans and red bell peppers creates a wonderful flavour. I first tasted this soup at a dinner party hosted by one of my best friends, Annabelle Bond. Today it is my favourite soup.

Serves 4.

3 small bell peppers (yellow, red and orange)

1 small onion, chopped

1 tablespoon olive oil

1 can (15 ounces/425 g) cannellini beans

4 dried red chillis, crushed

2 (10 ounces/280 g) cans chicken broth

First, grill the bell peppers (see page 39). Chop each bell pepper into small cubes.

Fry the onion in oil, add the bell peppers, then the beans and crushed chillies. Add the chicken broth. Cook till beans are tender. Cool, then purée. Serve cold.

Chickpea Curry Soup

This warm and hearty soup originates from Tenerife and is traditional to this area. I discovered this soup earlier this year whilst visiting my mother. It is incredibly filling and is a meal in itself.

$1^1/_2$ tablespoons vegetable oil

1 medium onion, chopped

1 medium green bell pepper, chopped

2 cloves garlic, crushed

$1^1/_2$ tablespoons curry powder

1 tablespoon malt vinegar

14 ounces/400 g canned tomatoes, crushed

$1^1/_2$ pounds/680 g chickpeas, rinsed, drained

3 medium potatoes, peeled, chopped

$^1/_3$ cup yoghurt

Heat the oil in a large saucepan. Cook the onion, bell pepper, garlic and curry powder, stirring until the onion is soft. Add the vinegar, undrained crushed tomatoes, chickpeas and potatoes. Cover and let simmer for about 20 minutes or until potatoes are tender, stirring occasionally. Top with yoghurt before serving.

Marsha's Artichoke Soup

The first time I ever tasted this recipe 12 years ago in Hong Kong, I nearly died and went to Heaven. Do remember to add plenty of water and sieve well to ensure all the tough fibres are removed from the artichoke.

Serves 4.

4 tablespoons butter

2 shallots, finely chopped

8 fresh artichoke bottoms

salt and pepper

4 tablespoons flour

5 cups chicken stock, heated

$^1/_2$ cup heavy cream

lemon juice

1 tablespoon chopped parsley

Heat the butter on medium heat and add shallots and artichokes. Season with salt and pepper. Cover and cook for 20 minutes on low heat. Mix in the flour and cook for a further 5 minutes. Pour in the chicken stock and stir thoroughly. Bring to the boil and cook for 20 minutes on low heat. Purée the soup, then stir in the cream and lemon juice. Serve with chopped parsley.

Curried Apple and Green Pea Soup

A strange combination of ingredients but the result is fabulous. Kindly provided by a wonderful friend, Deborah Morgan, this makes a terrific starter to any dinner party. Be warned: do make sure to make plenty, as guests will be asking for second helpings!

2 leeks (can substitute with 1 large onion)

1 ounce/30 g butter

3 level tablespoons mild curry powder or to taste

2 cups frozen or shelled peas (do not use mint-flavoured peas)

2 Granny Smith apples, peeled, cored and chopped

1 large (7 ounces/200 g) potato, peeled and chopped

6 cups chicken stock or water with a few sprigs of mint

2 teaspoons plain flour

1 cup milk

chopped chives or mint sprigs for garnish

1 apple to garnish (slice thin at last minute)

a little cream for serving (optional)

Trim the leeks, discarding the leaves. Halve the white portions lengthwise and rinse under cold water, tapping to remove dirt. Slice the leeks and fry gently in butter without browning, 5–10 minutes. Add the curry powder and cook a few more minutes. Add the peas, apple, potato, chicken stock and mint leaves. Cover and simmer until the vegetables are tender, about $1^1/_2$ hours, then purée in a food processor, and return to the saucepan.

Mix the flour with a little milk to smooth out any lumps, then add with the remaining milk to the soup. Stir constantly until the soup boils and is very smooth. Adjust the consistency if necessary by adding a little more milk or water.

Serve with a little swirl of cream and garnish with chives and/or mint and a fresh apple, thinly sliced. Serve with poppadums.

Smoked Bacon and Split Pea Soup

I first discovered these next two winter soups while recruiting for MBAs at Harvard University. One freezing day in Boston I stopped by a little café to warm up with a bowl of soup and this dish certainly did the trick. This wholesome, thick soup is a meal in itself. Serve piping hot.

Makes about 4 litres.

1/2 pound/225 g smoked bacon, diced

1 white onion, roughly chopped

1/8 cup chopped garlic

1 bay leaf

16 cups (8 pints/4 litres) chicken stock

2 pounds/910 g dried split green peas

Tabasco, salt and pepper for seasoning

Sweat the bacon until all fat is rendered out and bacon is crisp. Sauté the onion, garlic and bay leaf in bacon fat until the onion is transparent. Add the chicken stock and peas, then bring to the boil. Simmer until peas are cooked. Season with Tabasco, salt and pepper. Purée for one minute only so the soup remains thick and you can still see the bacon and pea parts.

Tomato Lentil Soup

1 cup boiled yellow lentils (boiled with salt)

1 onion, chopped

1 tablespoon oil

1 carrot, chopped

1 can (14 ounces/400 g) chopped Italian tomatoes

2 cans (28 ounces/800 g) chicken stock

salt and pepper

First boil the lentils with a little salt until soft. Set aside.

Sauté the chopped onion in 1 tablespoon oil in a deep saucepan for 3 minutes. Add the chopped carrot, then stir-fry for another 2 minutes. Stir in the chopped tomatoes, and boil for 5 minutes. Add the chicken stock and let it simmer for 20–25 minutes, or until the carrots are soft.

Add the cooked lentils, then season with salt and pepper. Serve hot.

This recipe mirrors a minestrone – thick and hearty. Serve with hot crusty rolls.

Gazpacho

This is one of the earliest recipes that I collected when visiting Cyprus. Too much garlic can spoil it but it does make a fulfilling lunch on a lovely hot day. Remember to serve it cold!

1 egg

2 cloves garlic

1 slice bread

dash of vinegar (preferably cider vinegar)

1 tablespoon oil

1 red pepper

1/2 cucumber

2 teaspoons tomato purée

1 can (14 ounces/400 g) tomato

2 cups tomato juice

2 spring onions

salt and pepper

Lea & Perrins Worcestershire sauce to taste

salad seasoning

2 drops Tabasco

Mix all the ingredients together and liquidise.

Mummy's Pumpkin Soup

I serve this every year at Thanksgiving and it guarantees a perfect result. I use an actual pumpkin shell to make lanterns for the table decorations.

Add as much as you like, depending on how many you are catering for, but for 8 people you need:

2–3 cloves garlic, chopped

2–3 onions, sliced

2–3 tomatoes, quartered

half a large pumpkin, cut into cubes

1 potato, cut into cubes

1 quart/1 litre water

3 chicken stock cubes

1 small can (6 ounces/170 g) tomato paste

pinch of sugar

salt and pepper to season

cream to taste

croutons

chopped parsley for garnish

Fry the garlic and the onion gently in oil until the onion is soft, then add fresh tomatoes.

Put the pumpkin and potato into about 1 quart/1 litre of water with the chicken stock, bring to the boil and simmer. When soft, add the cooked onions and tomatoes and the tomato paste and cook for another 10–20 minutes.

Liquidise. Add seasoning to taste, and add cream just before serving. Serve with croutons and chopped parsley.

Cyprus

PASTA & RICE

India

Black Pepper Fettuccine with Three-Cheese Sauce

Serves 4 or 6.

FOR THE BLACK PEPPER PASTA DOUGH

2 tablespoons black peppercorns

10 ounces/280 g strong plain flour, more if
    needed

3 eggs

1 tablespoon vegetable oil

1 teaspoon salt

FOR THE THREE-CHEESE SAUCE

4 ounces/110 g Gorgonzola cheese

6 fl. ounces/180 ml double cream

2 ounces/50 g grated Parmesan cheese

4 ounces/110 g Ricotta cheese

Put the peppercorns in a double thickness of plastic bags and crush with rolling pin. Alternatively, grind them coarsely in a pepper mill or electric coffee grinder or spice mill.

Make the pasta dough, adding the crushed pepper with the flour, eggs, oil and salt (alternatively, you can use store-bought pasta). Knead, roll out and cut the dough with a pasta machine, ending with the rollers at the narrowest setting and using the wider of the machine's cutters. Alternatively, knead, roll out and cut the dough by hand, rolling it out to the thickness of a postcard and cutting it into ¼ inch/6 mm wide strips. Toss the fettuccine gently with a little flour or fine cornmeal, then coil loosely in bundles or leave flat. Leave to dry on a floured tea towel for 1–2 hours.

Cut the Gorgonzola cheese into small pieces, discarding any rind. Put the cream in the saucepan and add the Gorgonzola, Parmesan and Ricotta. Heat gently, stirring, for 2–3 minutes until the cheese melts. Do not overheat.

Fill a large pan with water, bring to the boil and add 1 tablespoon of salt. Add the fettuccine and simmer about 1–2 minutes until tender but still chewy, stirring occasionally to prevent sticking. Drain the pasta in a colander, rinse with hot water to wash away the starch, and drain again. Transfer the hot pasta to a large warmed bowl, and pour cheese sauce over the pasta. Toss the fettuccine and cheese sauce together with large forks until all the pasta is coated with the sauce. Taste for seasoning and serve immediately.

Beetroot Ravioli with a Light Basil Sauce

Serves 4.

1 beetroot

2 eggs

4 ounces/110 g flour

3 tablespoons water

4 ounces/110 g Ricotta cheese

salt and black pepper

$^1/_2$ tablespoon Parmesan cheese, finely grated

nutmeg, freshly grated

2 tablespoons olive oil

4 ounces/110 g raw spinach, washed and stalks trimmed

FOR THE DRESSING

3 tablespoons pesto sauce

1 tablespoon fresh basil, finely chopped

1 tablespoon olive oil

To make the pasta, boil the beetroot in salted water until tender, then drain and peel. Cool and purée in the blender. Mix eggs and flour with water. Knead in the beetroot purée and let the dough rest for one hour.

Season the Ricotta cheese with salt, pepper, Parmesan cheese and nutmeg. Heat the olive oil in a pan and add spinach. Toss around until wilted. Add to the cheese mixture and whizz in the blender.

Roll the pasta as thinly as possible on a lightly floured board. Cut circles with a 2 inch/5 cm plain cutter. Place forkfuls of stuffing on pasta circles, dampen the edges and fold over, pressing to seal the edges. Cook in plenty of boiling salted water for 5 to 6 minutes. Drain and arrange the ravioli like a fan on plates.

FOR THE DRESSING

Mix the pesto sauce with basil and olive oil, then drizzle over the pasta before serving.

Pesto

Serves 4–6.

3 bunches fresh basil

1 tablespoon oil

2 tablespoons pinenuts

2 cloves garlic, peeled

salt and pepper

$^1/_4$ cup extra virgin olive oil

3 tablespoons grated Parmesan cheese

Wash the basil, removing the leaves from the stems and discarding the stems. You'll need about 2 cups of leaves.

Place the oil and pinenuts in a small saucepan, and cook over low heat until the pinenuts are a light golden brown, and drain immediately.

Place the basil leaves, pinenuts, peeled garlic, salt and pepper in a food processor fitted with a metal blade. Process until the mixture becomes smooth and is finely chopped. With the processor still going, add olive oil in a thin stream. Process a further 1 second. (You may also use a blender; stop the blender and scrape the mixture from the sides occasionally to ensure it all gets blended equally.)

Turn the basil mixture out into a bowl, add the Parmesan cheese, and mix until combined.

Harriet Usherwood's Vegetarian Lasagne

When my sister-in-law Harriet makes her vegetarian lasagne, the family loves it. Totally her own creation, this is simply delicious when served with homemade bread and a crisp salad.

1 red onion, chopped

1 tablespoon oil

1 red bell pepper, chopped

1/2 cup pinenuts (optional)

1 stalk celery, chopped

1 pound/450 g sliced courgettes

salt and pepper to taste

1 tin (14 ounces/400 g) chopped tomatoes

1 teaspoon brown sugar

1 cup boiling water

1 clove crushed garlic

1/4 pound/110 g fresh spinach

6 pieces pasta sheets

1 cup grated cheese

FOR THE WHITE SAUCE

4 tablespoons butter

1 ounce/30 g plain flour

2–2 1/2 cups milk

salt and pepper

dash of ground nutmeg

Sauté the chopped onion in oil, then add the chopped red bell pepper. (I sometimes add a handful of pinenuts here.) Stir-fry for 3 minutes. Add the celery and courgettes. Stir-fry, then add salt and pepper to taste. Add the tin of chopped tomatoes, add a teaspoonful of sugar, boil for 5 minutes, then add 1 cup of boiling water. Simmer for 10 minutes or until there's just enough juice left to cook the pasta, then add the garlic. Stir in the fresh spinach, then set aside.

Meanwhile, for the white sauce, melt the butter in a separate saucepan. Add the flour and stir for 2 minutes. Slowly add the milk, stirring continuously until creamy, then add salt and pepper and a dash of ground nutmeg.

In an 8 inch x 8 inch/20 cm x 20 cm baking tin or ovenproof glass dish, lay a pasta sheet, then add a layer of vegetable, then a layer of white sauce, and then sprinkle cheese on top. Repeat with the second and third layer.

Bake in a 400°F/200°C/Gas 6 preheated oven for 15–20 minutes or until golden brown on top.

Katharine Pooley's
Homemade Lasagne

There is nothing more enjoyable than relaxing with a TV dinner at home. This is no ordinary lasagne, as you will discover, but my favourite relaxation meal when I just feel like curling up and switching off.

2 cloves garlic, minced

3 tablespoons olive oil

1 onion, chopped

1 pound/450 g minced steak

dash of cayenne pepper

1 cup frozen sweet peas

1/2 cup Heinz tomato ketchup

2 cups chopped canned tomato

1 cup fresh cherry tomatoes

1 tablespoon Lea & Perrins Worcestershire sauce

salt and pepper to taste

FOR WHITE SAUCE

3 ounces/85 g butter

1 ounce/30 g plain flour

2 cups fresh milk

dash of ground nutmeg

1 tablespoon Lea & Perrins Worcestershire sauce

1/2 cup grated cheese

salt and pepper to taste

9 sheets (not pre-cooked) lasagne sheets

1/2 cup grated Parmesan cheese

1/2 cup grated Mozzarella or Cheddar cheese

In a deep saucepan, sauté the minced garlic in olive oil until brown, then add chopped onion. Fry for 3 minutes, add minced beef and stir-fry until brown, then add a dash of cayenne pepper. Stir in the sweet peas, add tomato ketchup, chopped tomatoes and fresh cherry tomatoes. Stir-fry and add 1 1/2 cups water and boil for 15 minutes on medium heat. Season with Worcestershire sauce, salt and pepper. Set aside, and make the white sauce.

To make the white sauce, in another saucepan, melt the butter. Add the plain flour and stir for 3 minutes. Add the milk slowly and continue stirring until creamy. Add a dash of ground nutmeg, a tablespoon of Worcestershire sauce, grated cheese, salt and pepper to taste.

In a 9 x 13 inch/23 x 33 cm baking dish spread a small amount of meat sauce. Layer with 3 lasagne sheets, then one layer of meat sauce, then white sauce, then a sprinkling of cheese. Do the same with the second and third layers. Bake for 20–25 minutes in a 400°F/200°C/ Gas 6 oven.

Katharine in Ecuador with Sally's dogs

Katy de Tilly's Vodka Pasta

This wonderful pasta recipe was passed on by a friend from Hong Kong called Katy de Tilly, who happened to be holding an art exhibition at her house when serving this meal. I am not sure if it was the culinary art of the pasta or the amount of vodka in it that encouraged me to buy several of her paintings! Go easy with the vodka!

2 (14 ounces/400 g) cans tomatoes (Pelati or other Italian ones)

1/2 cup olive oil

salt to taste

3 chillies (small, hot ones, chopped)

2 tablespoons vodka

cream

Parmesan cheese

pasta (cook according to package instructions)

Cook the tomatoes slowly on low heat, with a good amount of olive oil and salt, for 1 1/2–2 hours while marinating the chillies in the vodka. Mix with the tomatoes until you have boiled out the vodka. Add a small amount of cream and Parmesan cheese and slowly stir in the pasta until evenly distributed. Serve piping hot.

Pineapple Fried Rice

Pineapple Fried Rice

Serves 4–6.

1 pineapple

2 tablespoons vegetable oil

1 small onion, sliced

2 green chillies, seeded and chopped

8 ounces/225 g lean pork, diced small

4 ounces/110 g cooked shelled shrimp

3–4 cups cooked cold rice

1/2 cup roasted cashew nuts

2 scallions, chopped

2 tablespoons fish sauce

1 tablespoon dark soy sauce

2 red chillies, sliced

1 green chilli, sliced

Cut the pineapple in half lengthwise and remove the flesh. Keep about 4 ounces/110 g of the fruit, chopped finely.

Heat the oil in a wok. Add the onion and chillies and fry for 4 minutes until soft. Add the pork and cook till brown on all sides.

Stir in the shrimp and rice and toss well together. Continue to fry until the rice is thoroughly heated.

Add the chopped pineapple, cashew nuts and scallions. Season with fish sauce and dark soy sauce.

Spoon into the pineapple shells. Garnish with sliced chillies. Serve in the shells.

Prague

Tagliatelle with Ham au Gratin

1 tablespoon salt

3 tablespoons unsalted butter

1$^1/_2$ cups prosciutto (Italian ham, specialty of Parma), cut into julienne strips

$^3/_4$ pound/340 g dried tagliatelle (egg pasta)

$^1/_2$ cup freshly grated Parmesan cheese, plus extra to pass around the table

$^1/_2$ cup Béchamel Sauce (recipe follows)

Preheat the oven.

Bring a large pot of water to the boil and add a tablespoon of salt.

Melt 1 tablespoon of the butter in a large skillet over medium-high heat. Add the ham and cook for a minute or two, stirring constantly. Cook the pasta in the boiling water for two minutes or until *al dente*. Drain well in a colander, and put it in the skillet. Toss with the ham, add another tablespoon of butter, sprinkle with half the Parmesan and toss well.

Spread the pasta evenly in a 2-quart/ 2-litre ovenproof casserole. Spoon the sauce over the top and sprinkle with the remaining Parmesan. Cut the remaining butter into bits and scatter over the top. Broil as close as possible to the heat source until golden and bubbly, about 1 to 2 minutes. Serve immediately and pass around a small bowl of grated Parmesan cheese.

BÉCHAMEL SAUCE

Serves 4–6.

15 fl. ounces/440 ml milk

1 small piece carrot

$^1/_2$ smallish onion

celery (2 inches/5 cm)

6 whole black peppercorns

ground nutmeg to taste

$^1/_2$ bay leaf

1 ounce/30 g butter

1 ounce/30 g flour

5 fl. ounces/150 ml single or double cream

Place the milk in a saucepan with the carrot, onion, celery, peppercorns, ground nutmeg and bay leaf, then bring to the boil very slowly. After that, remove from the heat and allow it to infuse for 20 minutes. Strain the milk into a jug and make the sauce by adding the butter and flour. Finish off with the single or double cream, depending on how creamy you want it. Alternatively, you can use 10 fl. ounces/300 ml of white wine instead of milk to infuse the ingredients.

Sweet Pea Ravioli with Pinenuts and Mascarpone Cheese

While on an all-girls tour with Annabelle and Lucy Bond, Marguerite Krikhaar and Lisa Tseng in Los Angeles, I discovered this wonderful recipe. I cook it as a starter – more than four pieces of ravioli each and it becomes too rich.

FOR THE FILLING

2 cups small grade A peas, lightly blanched in salted water

1/4 cup toasted pinenuts

1/4 cup Mascarpone cheese

1/8 cup grated Parmesan cheese

salt and white pepper to taste

FOR DOUGH

1 cup all-purpose flour

1 egg

1 yolk

pinch of salt

spot of water

spot of extra virgin olive oil

FOR SAUCE

1 pound/450 g unsalted butter

20 sage leaves, sliced thin

1 cup sherry vinegar

To make the filling, blend all the filling ingredients in a food processor or blender to a semi-smooth consistency, then set aside in the refrigerator.

Next, make the dough. Blend all the dough ingredients except water and oil in a food processor until completely incorporated. Add water and oil (1–2 teaspoons maximum) to make it hold together. Set aside for 2–3 hours to relax the gluten, then make the ravioli with heaping amounts of the filling.

For the sauce, heat the butter in a saucepan until slightly browned, whisking the butter. Remove from heat and pour into a metal mixing bowl, then add the sage leaves, whisking the whole time. Add the sherry vinegar and whisk until the sauce cools significantly.

When all this is done, heat four pieces of ravioli, and add the fresh English peas to the water, so when you remove the ravioli you also remove the peas at the same time.

Serve with the brown butter sauce and pea shoots.

SAUCES, DRESSINGS & JAMS

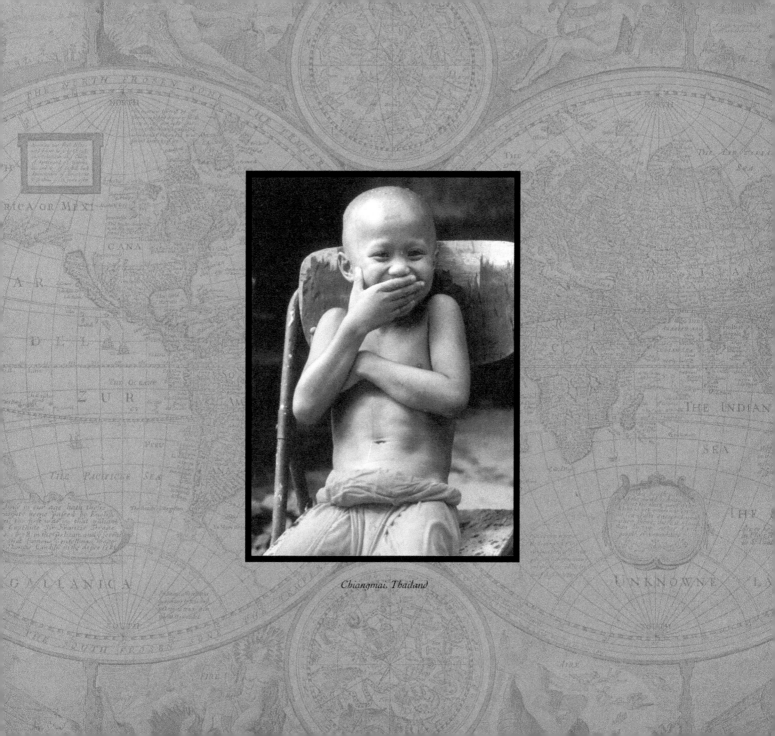

Chiangmai, Thailand

Julian Pooley's Infamous Gravy

My brother Julian would literally turn in his grave if he found out that I am passing on this recipe but due to much demand from friends wanting to know the secret, I have relented. It contains the most unusual ingredients but the result is a rich, tasty gravy guaranteed to bring alive a roast dinner.

1 teaspoon mustard (any kind will do)

1 cup water

2 teaspoons tomato ketchup

2 tablespoons Bovril

1 teaspoon horseradish sauce

1 teaspoon Lea & Perrins Worcestershire sauce

a little plain flour to thicken

1/4 cup red or white wine (sometimes I add sherry)

Place all the ingredients into a large tea mug and stir together vigorously. Fill the mug to the brim with hot water and stir gently, allowing everything to melt. Pour the liquid into a saucepan. Bring to the boil and slowly simmer for around 20 minutes. I often make this when I am cooking a roast, whether beef, lamb, chicken or pork. Once you are ready to carve, pour all the juices left over from the roast (including any fat) into the gravy. It may look as though there is a lot of oil or fat but this is only natural animal fat and once you bring it to the boil again it will cook itself. Add the wine. Bring to the boil slowly and then turn down the heat and simmer gently for another 10–15 minutes. Add flour to thicken if necessary. (You must do this by adding the flour with water first, otherwise the gravy will become lumpy.)

Red Wine Sauce

The following three sauces – Red Wine, Truffle Cream and Parmesan – all come from the head chef at one of the top hotels in Hong Kong. All require a great deal of patience and cooking time but the results are mouthwatering and worth it.

Prepares 1 cup.

2 large red onions, peeled and roughly sliced

1 1/2 fl. ounces/40 ml vegetable oil

1 teaspoon sugar

1 teaspoon salt

1 sprig thyme

1 sprig rosemary

4 cloves garlic

4 bay leaves

1 small potato, peeled and grated

1 cup red wine

1 cup veal jus (store-bought)

3/4 ounce/20 g butter

Roast the onion in vegetable oil with sugar and salt and cook until soft, but do not let it brown. Once soft, add the thyme, rosemary, garlic, bay leaves, grated potato and red wine. Reduce to a quarter before adding veal jus and butter. Simmer gently for about 1 hour, then pass through a fine sieve. Season to taste and freeze in an ice cube tray to keep. Fantastic with red meat and veal.

Truffle Cream Sauce

10 ounces/280 g butter

1 cup truffle juice

2 ounces/50 g potato purée

a few drops reduced Madeira (1 bottle to 3 1/3 fl. ounces/100 ml), to taste

salt and pepper

whipped cream (optional)

Melt the butter in a saucepan and add the remaining ingredients, then simmer gently for about 1 hour. Add salt and pepper to taste.

Add some whipped cream at the end if it is meant for pasta. Blend with a hand mixer if it is to be used as a sauce for meat or fish.

Parmesan Sauce

1 cup chicken stock, reduced from 4 cups stock

7 ounces/200 g butter

7 ounces/200 g Parmesan cheese, grated

3 1/3 fl. ounces/100 ml cream

Add all the ingredients and mix well. Simmer for 1 hour. Season to taste.

Istanbul

Cradle Mountain Tomato and Passionfruit Jam

Cradle Mountain Tomato and Passionfruit Jam

This very unusual combination of tomatoes and passionfruit makes a remarkable jam and is best served on fresh hot scones. I discovered this recipe while staying at Cradle Mountain Lodge in Tasmania, Australia.

$6^2/_3$ pounds/3 kg Roma tomatoes

$2^1/_4$ pounds/1 kg apples, peeled, cored and finely diced

$3^1/_3$ fl. ounces/100 ml lemon juice

1 pound/450 g fresh passionfruit pulp (or canned pulp)

10 pounds/$4^1/_2$ kg sugar

2 tablespoons citric acid

Ayers Rock, Australia

The tomatoes should be firm and just ripe. Skin, de-seed and chop them coarsely. To peel the tomatoes, cut a small cross on top of each and submerge them in boiling water for 30–45 seconds, then refresh in ice water. The skin should peel off easily. Cut in half and remove seeds.

In a large stainless steel pot, simmer the diced apples with the lemon juice until soft, then add the tomatoes and passionfruit pulp. Bring to the boil. Add sugar and citric acid and stir with a metal spoon until the sugar is well dissolved. Simmer on low heat until the jam reaches the desired consistency; test by putting small amounts of jam onto a saucer and refrigerating.

Pour the jam hot into sterilised glass jars, refrigerate and seal the jars when cold.

Pineapple Salsa

1 cup very ripe peeled, cored and diced pineapple

2 teaspoons dark brown sugar

1 teaspoon unseasoned rice vinegar

2 chillies or 2 canned chipotle chillies, chopped very fine

$1/_2$ cup finely chopped sweet red bell peppers

juice of 1 Mexican lime

1 tablespoon finely minced cilantro/coriander

1 shallot, chopped fine

Mix all the ingredients together, taste, add more lime juice and chillies as needed. This is perfect served as a side sauce at barbecues.

Artichoke Parmesan Dip

14 ounce/400 g can artichoke hearts, drained

4 large cloves garlic, chopped

1 tablespoon lemon juice

$1/4$ cup mayonnaise

$1/4$ cup soft cream cheese

$1/2$ cup Parmesan cheese

In a food processor, pulse together the artichoke and garlic, then mix in the other ingredients. Place in a casserole dish and sprinkle with Parmesan cheese.

Bake at 375°F/190°C/Gas 5 for 20 minutes.

Angela Edward's Vinaigrette

This is the secret of my everyday salad dressing – it never fails and all my friends comment on how good it tastes on any type of salad.

3 tablespoons olive oil

3 tablespoons gourmet vinegar

1 tablespoon brown sugar

1 tablespoon seed mustard

generous shake of Parmesan cheese

parsley, chopped

chives, chopped

Mix all the ingredients together in a tight container and shake well until all ingredients are smoothly blended. Best served with a light crisp salad.

Chicken Jus

$31/3$ pounds/$11/2$ kg chicken bones

2 fl. ounces/60 ml sunflower oil

2 ounces/50 g butter

2 ounces/50 g mirepoix (celery roots/onions/ carrots)

1 tablespoon tomato paste

1 clove garlic, roughly chopped

$3/4$ cup red wine

$3/4$ cup white wine

$3/4$ cup Madeira

10 cups water

2 bay leaves

5 peppercorns

1 teaspoon salt

Chop the chicken bones as small as possible. Heat a roasting tray and heat the sunflower oil. Add the bones and roast, turning from time to time to ensure even colouring. Once the bones are an even dark brown, add the butter and mirepoix, mixing them well together. Roast for another 5 minutes before adding tomato paste and garlic. Roast for 10 minutes, then start to add wines and Madeira one by one. Make sure that the alcohol is poured evenly all over the bones, especially if the bones are sticking to the pan.

Transfer everything to a large pot and cover with cold water. Ensure that all residue is transferred. Bring to the boil and skim. Simmer gently and add the bay leaves, peppercorns and salt. Cook for about 4 hours. Pass through a cheesecloth and reduce to taste.

Peanut Sauce

BLEND IN FOOD PROCESSOR

1 tablespoon yellow onion, chopped

1 clove minced garlic

1 tablespoon peanut oil

$2^1/_2$ tablespoons soy sauce

$1^1/_2$ tablespoons lime juice

pinch of cayenne pepper

TRANSFER TO A BOWL AND WHISK IN

2 tablespoons brown sugar

1 teaspoon molasses

$^1/_2$ cup creamy peanut butter

$^1/_4$ cup water

pinch of more cayenne

Rosemary Honey Dressing

This light salad dressing comes from Blanket Bay Hotel in New Zealand. It makes a refreshing change from a balsamic vinaigrette.

WHISK TOGETHER

4 tablespoons soy sauce

2 tablespoons honey

dash of white wine vinegar

5 fl. ounces/150 ml grapeseed oil

chopped rosemary

freshly ground pepper

Adjust any of the ingredients to your taste. Goes perfectly with a light salad.

Vietnamese Table Sauce

This recipe makes just over $^3/_4$ cup sauce.

$^1/_4$ cup fresh lime juice

$^1/_4$ cup Vietnamese or Thai fish sauce

$^1/_4$ cup water

2 teaspoons rice or cider vinegar

1 tablespoon sugar

1 small clove garlic, minced

1 bird chilli, minced

several shreds of carrot (optional)

Combine all the ingredients in a bowl and stir to dissolve the sugar completely. Serve in one or more small condiment bowls. Store in a tightly sealed glass container in the refrigerator for up to 3 days. After that, the garlic starts to taste tired.

Cambodia

CHILDREN OF CAMBODIA

Cambodia – this previously war-torn country, site of the killing fields and the grave of Pol Pot, one of the 20th century's most infamous mass murderers, is slowly getting back into business gear with the return of the tourists. Life has new meaning for the Cambodians; peace is what they need and want.

Despite the emerging attractions, I was in Cambodia for a different purpose. Working in Hong Kong, I had heard about the plight of Cambodian children orphaned by the war. So I started a drive to collect as many toys as I could, with the intention of visiting a children's home north of Phnom Penh, the capital. Flying to Angkor Wat was the fastest way to reach my destination, and from there, bearing medical supplies, toys and other goodies, I drove out to the countryside.

The young ones were in a state of excitement when I arrived at the home, which was clean and simple. Once I had separated the toys into piles according to age group, the children gleefully zoomed in on their favourites. It was both poignant and gratifying to see the delight on their faces – brought on by nothing more than a small gift.

Mission accomplished, I took the opportunity to explore the magnificent temples of Angkor Wat. This historic settlement, dating back to the 8th century, was discovered by French botanist Henri Mahout in 1860, proving true the local legend about a lost city in the forest. The buildings, monuments in themselves, have withstood the ravages of war, and are an apt symbol of the Cambodian spirit. I would not hesitate to return to this charming piece of Asia, armed again with bags of toys.

FISH

Bhutan

Remy Madriaga's Salmon with Teriyaki Sauce

This is one of the popular dishes we eat at home. Remy cooks the salmon just right so that it crumbles off the fork. The accompanying sauce is very rich so only a small amount is needed, but it is totally delicious.

6 tablespoons Mitsukan cooking rice wine

6 tablespoons Kikkoman milder soy sauce

5 tablespoons Japanese Takara Hon-Mirin (sweet sake)

1 tablespoon sugar

6 slices salmon fillet (1 inch/2¹/₂ cm thick)

1 tablespoon butter

Boil all the ingredients except the salmon and butter in a saucepan until the sugar dissolves, then leave aside. Fry the salmon fillet with butter for one minute on each side, then add the teriyaki sauce mixture to the salmon and boil to thicken the sauce. Serve with rice and stir-fried vegetables.

Smoked Trout Pâté

This is one of my earliest recipes, where I used to have time to decorate each course. It is simple to do, just time-consuming, but the result is eye-catching at a fun dinner party.

Serves 4.

2 smoked trout

1 teaspoon lemon juice

¹/₂ teaspoon creamed horseradish

1 cup double cream

1 egg white

4 slices smoked salmon

cucumber slices and dill, to garnish

2 tablespoons vinaigrette dressing

Remove the heads and tails from the trout and split the heads and tails in half. Take the skin off the fish and discard along with the bones.

Process the trout flesh in a blender or food processor to a paste. Add the lemon juice and horseradish. Pour in the cream with the machine still running and process to a soft creamy paste. Beat the egg white until stiff and fold in.

Divide the pâté between the smoked salmon slices and roll into a cylinder, fatter at one end than the other, like the body of a fish.

Snip the half tails and use them and the half-heads to garnish. Arrange the fish in a sea of cucumber slices, tossed in the vinaigrette dressing, and garnish with dill.

Guilin, China

Everest

EVEREST BASE CAMP

Mountains have always attracted me, and Mount Everest has beckoned since my childhood. While I have gone trekking and exploring in Nepal and Everest Base Camp many times, the trip I recall most vividly is when I organised a group of ten friends, including my father and my 11-year-old godson. After an hour's flight in a 14-seater propeller plane, we landed in Lukla, at 9,350 feet, on a tiny uphill runway wedged amongst huge granite ridges. We were to spend the next ten days living the simple life of the Nepalese.

We made a night stop at Namche Bazaar, at 11,300 feet, to help us acclimatise to the altitude. Namche is the main trading centre for the Khumbu region, and being the weekly market-day, it was buzzing with people selling vegetables, and live chickens that squawked at the top of their lungs, oblivious to their fate. Our sherpas shopped furiously for supplies to carry on their backs over the next few days. We were woken at 6.00 each morning as they brought tea for us to our tents so we could admire the wonderful scenery in the comfort of our sleeping bags. All the meals were prepared by the sherpas who miraculously produced wonderfully succulent food, served in little dishes. Amazingly, they even made a chocolate cake for my godson who turned 12 the day before we reached Base Camp.

To cope with the altitude, we climbed very slowly to Thangboche at 12,700 feet, where to our surprise we came across a team of monks engaged in a cricket match. We joined in, but alas, they easily won.

My habit of stocking my rucksack with my own secret stash of goodies (Ribena, Bovril, plenty of biscuits) was much appreciated by everyone on the trek. The biscuits made great handouts for the hordes of children who always gathered round, giggling and peeking at us.

The Everest Base Camp Trek is not as easy as it sounds. At 17,200 feet, nothing is easy. Teamwork is the order of the day. Even with such a large group, this expedition proved highly successful, with everyone having a great time. I feel privileged to have had the opportunity to witness the immense power this mountain commands. I now have a pressing plan to climb Mount Everest, but whether this burning ambition will be fulfilled remains to be seen.

Prawn Cocktail Ice Bowl

Prawn Cocktail Ice Bowl

This is another well-tried recipe. It does require a few hours' preparation but it always guarantees success at dinner parties. You will need to prepare the ice bowls the day before, and in order for the bowls not to melt you should serve this starter immediately.

Serves 6.

FOR THE ICE BOWL

6 dill fronds

1 small lemon, sliced

FOR THE PRAWN COCKTAIL

2 tablespoons double cream

4 tablespoons mayonnaise

1 tablespoon tomato purée

cayenne pepper

2 tablespoons lemon juice

1 small galia or ogen melon

1 small red bell pepper, sliced

1 red apple, diced

4 small stalks celery, sliced

1 pound/450 g prawns, thawed if frozen

6 leaves curly endive

paprika pepper

6 whole prawns, to garnish

Fill a 8$\frac{1}{2}$ inch/22 cm bowl one third full of very cold water. Put an 7 inch/18 cm bowl inside the first and secure with tape. Push the dill fronds between the two bowls, making sure they are just covered with water. Freeze. Add the lemon slices, top up with cold water and freeze again.

Meanwhile, make the prawn cocktail. Whip the cream and mix it with the mayonnaise, tomato purée, cayenne pepper and lemon juice. Using a melon baller, scoop the melon into balls. Mix them, together with the red bell pepper, apple, celery and prawns, with half the mayonnaise mixture.

Unmould the ice bowl and line it with the curly endive leaves. Put the prawn cocktail mixture on top of the leaves, top with the rest of the mayonnaise mixture and sprinkle with paprika. Garnish with the whole prawns and serve at once.

TIP: If the ice bowl cracks when it is unmoulded, just re-freeze it.

TO MAKE ICE BOWLS, YOU WILL NEED

2 containers of the same shape, one slightly smaller than the other

2 broad elastic bands or sticky tape

flowers, fruit, herbs, etc, for decoration

Fill the larger bowl one third full with cold tap water or still mineral water. Push the smaller bowl into the water and secure with the elastic bands or sticky tape, ensuring that the two bowl rims are level. The water should now come about two-thirds of the way up the bowls.

Push the decorations into the water between the bowls. Place the bowls in the freezer overnight or until frozen.

Add another layer of decorations and gently pour in a cupful of very cold water or enough to just cover the decorations. Freeze again. Then fill to the top with more iced water and freeze again.

To unmould the bowl, fill the smaller bowl with tepid water, twist to loosen and remove. Dip the bottom of the larger bowl in tepid water to loosen, then remove this too. Make sure the water isn't too hot or the bowl will crack. Keep the ice bowl in the freezer until required.

TIPS: To serve 4 people with a starter or dessert, use a 6 inch/15 cm bowl and a 7$\frac{1}{2}$ inch/19 cm bowl. To serve 6–8 people, use a 8 inch/20 cm bowl and a 9$\frac{1}{2}$ inch/24 cm bowl. To make individual ice bowls, use yoghurt, cottage cheese or coleslaw containers.

Glass bowls will allow you to see the pattern as you arrange it, but plastic bowls are easier to unmould.

A few drops of food colouring will tint the water a pale pink, green or orange. Select decorations for their shape and size: rose petals, leaves, mint leaves, dill fronds, starfruit, kiwi fruit, lemons and limes, strawberries and blackcurrants make colourful containers.

Before freezing ice bowls, check that there are no air bubbles as these will melt and produce a hole.

Pagan, Myanmar

Garfish with Lime and Caper Butter Sauce

Serves 4–6.

$1^1/_4$ pounds/560 g pink fir potatoes, in thick slices

2 tablespoons extra virgin olive oil

2 tablespoons lime juice

1 tablespoon chopped fresh thyme (optional)

cracked black pepper

18 garfish fillets (any other firm-fleshed white fish will do)

2 tablespoons salted baby capers, rinsed

$3^1/_2$ ounces/100 g unsalted cultured butter

Steam the potatoes until just tender and keep warm. Combine the olive oil, lime juice, thyme and a generous amount of pepper in a shallow non-metallic dish. Add the garfish slices and turn to coat in the mixture. Set aside for 5 minutes.

Heat a large frying pan, drain the fish fillets and cook in the hot pan for 1–2 minutes on each side or until just cooked through. Remove the fish from the pan and keep warm. Reduce the heat, add the remaining marinade, capers and butter, and cook until the butter turns a nutty brown.

To serve, pile the potatoes onto serving plates, top with the garfish fillets, drizzle with the sauce and serve at once.

Stir-Fried King Fish Thai Style

$14^1/_2$ ounces/410 g king fish (snapper or any other firm-fleshed white fish will do)

4 green bird chillies (or 2 red chillies)

Thai basil

1 fl. ounce/30 ml fish stock

2 cloves garlic

$1^1/_3$ fl. ounces/40 ml fish sauce (nam pla), or light soy sauce

$8^1/_2$ ounces/240 g steamed rice

Cut the fish into medallions about $^1/_2$ inch/1 cm thick and $1^1/_4$ inches/3 cm in diameter. Finely slice the bird chillies (or shred the red chillies if using). Shred the basil.

Heat the wok or heavy frying pan until hot but not smoking. Add the fish stock and crushed garlic, stirring continuously to prevent burning. When the garlic is cooked, add the fish and continue to fry for 3–4 minutes, being careful not to break up the fish. Add chilli, basil and fish sauce. Mix well to coat the fish, and serve immediately with steamed rice.

Cheesy Smoked Haddock and Prawn Tarts

Cheesy Smoked Haddock and Prawn Tarts

Makes 8 tarts.

shortcrust pastry (made of 8 ounces/225 g
    plain flour and 4 ounces/110 g butter)

8 ounces/225 g smoked haddock fillet

1 bay leaf

3 black peppercorns

milk (enough to cover fillet in the pan)

7 ounces/200 g raw freshwater or
    Madagascan prawns

1 tablespoon olive oil

2 tablespoons lemon juice

1 ounce/30 g coarsely grated Gruyère cheese

3 tablespoons finely chopped parsley

2 egg yolks

9^1/$_2$ fl. ounces/280 ml double cream

pinch of cayenne pepper

salt and freshly ground black pepper

Preheat the oven to 400°F/200°C/Gas 6. Roll out the pastry on a lightly floured surface, then line eight 3^1/$_2$ inch/9 cm diameter quiche tins. Prick the bottom of each with a fork. Line with greaseproof paper and fill with baking beans. Chill for 30 minutes.

Place the pastry cases in the centre of the preheated oven and bake blind for 12 minutes. Remove from the oven and discard the weighted paper. Reduce the oven temperature to 350°F/180°C/Gas 4.

Meanwhile, cut the smoked haddock fillet in half and place in a saucepan with the bay leaf and peppercorns. Cover with milk. Set over low heat to simmer. Poach the fish for about 5 minutes or until just cooked. Remove from the milk. When cool enough to handle, remove the skin and any hidden bones and break flesh into chunks. Set aside in a bowl.

Peel the prawn tails, then make a small incision down the length of their backs and remove the dark cord. Rinse under cold running water and pat dry. Heat the oil in a small frying pan over medium-high heat. Add the prawns and fry briskly until pink. Remove, cut into large pieces and mix into the fish. Mix in lemon juice, followed by cheese and parsley.

Beat the egg yolks with a fork; stir into the cream. Mix into the fish and season to taste with cayenne pepper, salt and freshly ground black pepper. Divide the mixture between the tart cases. Return to the oven and bake for 25 minutes or until the filling is just set and golden brown.

Bhutan

BIRTHDAY IN BHUTAN

Beautiful Bhutan, a country of high mountains and deep valleys about the size of Switzerland, is located in the eastern Himalayas, sandwiched between India and Tibet. The country is unique. For one thing, it is the only country in the world to practise a Tantric form of Mahayana Buddhism. It is also a democratic monarchy run by a modern-day king. Tourism is strictly controlled in order to safeguard the country's biodiversity and ecosystems, and to protect the Bhutanese from the influences of the outside world. My mother, Didi, and I entered Bhutan as part of an escorted group.

The Bhutanese are extremely good-looking, and are proud of their country. They play an active role in preserving their traditions. They speak Dzongkha, a language similar to a Tibetan dialect, but many of them also learn English from an early age, and love to use it, becoming quite fluent as they grow older. They all wear the national dress, down to the tiniest child. The men wear the *gho*, which resembles a woven tartan dressing gown with white sleeves and a sash, the different colours of the sash denoting the rank of the wearer. The women wear *kira*, ankle-length dresses made from woven textiles in traditional patterns.

Expecting the worst in Bhutan, I had brought along my sleeping bag, but I was pleasantly surprised. The accommodation was excellent – each room had snug duvets and its own crackling fire at night. I had also brought some tins of sweet corn as a precaution against hunger pangs, but the food was fantastic, with fresh vegetables, curries and beef stews. I was reminded a great deal of Scotland.

Thinking that it would be almost impossible to have any night life in such a simple, quiet country, I joked with our handsome guide: "Where are all the nightclubs?" To my surprise, he did know of some, and seemed quite insistent on taking me to one. I politely declined. Later that night, something in my Lonely Planet guide caught my eye. It said, "Female travellers should be aware that romantic liaisons between tourists and Bhutanese guides are quite common. You might be invited to a nightclub or a party at the home of a Bhutanese male, only to discover too late that you are the only guest!"

This is just one precious memory I have of a fascinating country.

MEATS

Tanzania, Africa

DOG RACING, ALASKAN STYLE

Among the talented and interesting people I met in Anchorage, Alaska are two commercial pilots married to each other and to a fascinating sport – dog sledding. At Diana and Bruce Moroney's home I met the forty Alaskan huskies known personally to them. Most of the dogs are related to each other, all in some way descendants of Ruby, Diana's lead dog from the 1980s. They live in individual houses where, delightfully, they sit on top, looking at one another.

Dog sledding is very popular in Alaska as a competitive sport, and one of the most famous dog sledding events is the Iditarod Trail Sled Dog Race in March from Anchorage to Nome, a distance of 1,100 miles (1,800 kilometres). This annual event commemorates a desperate race by dog-sled teams to deliver diphtheria serum to Nome when the town was hit by an epidemic in 1925. The weather was so bad then that airplanes could not take off safely.

Each dog-sled team consists of tremendously fit canine athletes, well trained to take on the Alaskan weather and terrain that the race exposes them to. The race takes anywhere from nine to fifteen days to complete. It is important to have a good lead dog with a sixth sense of where the safe snow and ice lie. Just as important is the lead dog's rapport with and understanding of the musher's verbal commands. Up to sixteen dogs are used in a team during a race, and the musher must finish the race with five dogs.

Mushers must organise and ship out supplies to sustain themselves and the teams for the entire race. Outside assistance is not allowed. Once the race has begun a musher may "drop" a dog from his team at an official checkpoint, but dogs may not be added to the team.

When not competing in the race, both Diana and Bruce fly the trail as Iditarod Air Force Pilots. Iditarod Air Force flies support for the race by moving supplies, race personnel, veterinarians, race judges and dropped dogs in and out of the twenty checkpoints along the trail. Diana first started racing her Alaskan huskies in 1981 and has raced in nine Iditarods, her best finish being fourteenth in 1987. When we met, Bruce had run the race twice. It was a wonderful experience for me to learn more about dog sledding as I love dogs and have four of my own. How wonderful it must be to have forty!

Alaska

Liz Seaton's Braised Lamb Shanks

I first tasted this recipe in Hong Kong at a dinner party thrown by a friend, Janet Shafran. It was created, however, by Liz Seaton, owner of Gingers Catering Business, who is about to publish her own cookbook. I have used this dish at several successful dinner parties. The key to success is allowing the lamb to cook for a long time, so that it literally falls off your fork.

Serves 4.

The lamb shanks can be cooked a day before, then reheated.

4 lamb shanks
1 onion, chopped
1 carrot, chopped
1 stalk celery, chopped
parsley stalks
1 teaspoon salt

Place the shanks in a large pan, cover with water, and add vegetables and salt. Bring to the boil, then simmer for $2^{1}/_{2}$–3 hours till tender.

Transfer the shanks to an ovenproof dish and strain the stock into a container. Pour a cup of stock over the shanks to keep them moist. When ready to serve, warm for 15 minutes at high heat.

Pour the warmed sauce over shanks and serve.

FOR THE SAUCE

1 tablespoon oil
2 ounces/50 g butter
2 ounces/50 g plain flour
1 tablespoon tomato purée
1 glass red wine
$^{1}/_{2}$ the remaining stock

Heat the oil and butter, add the flour, and cook for a few minutes. Gradually add tomato purée, red wine and stock, then simmer for 20 minutes. Serve over hot lamb with mashed potatoes.

Mummy's Braised Beef

Everyone has a recipe that they associate with home and this one does just that for me. It is best served with roast potatoes and garden peas on a cold day, as this dish is very warm and filling. The longer you allow the beef to cook, the more the flavour will be enhanced, and the more tender the meat will become.

1–2 pounds/450–910 g beef, thickly cut, not cubes, preferably with a little fat on

flour

2–3 onions, thinly sliced

2–3 cloves garlic, crushed

1 teaspoon sugar

2–3 Oxo cubes

1 tablespoon dried or canned pimentos (red, green or mixed)

1 small can (6 ounces/170 g) tomato paste

4–6 bay leaves

crushed peppercorns or coarsely ground black pepper

1 sachet bouquet garni

Roll the meat in flour and place in a deep casserole dish layered with onion slices and crushed garlic.

In a jug, mix the sugar and Oxo cubes in a little hot water, then add the pimentos, tomato paste, bay leaves, peppercorns and bouquet garni. Pour over the meat, adding more water as the cooking will deplete the liquid.

Cook in the oven at 350°F/180°C/Gas 4 for 2–3 hours. You will know when it is done by piercing the meat with a fork – it should just break apart. If it does not, continue cooking, but do not overcook so that the meat breaks completely. It should flake with a fork when touched. Add any extra seasoning needed. Serve with garden peas and roast potatoes as Mummy makes, and phone Mummy to come over!

Beef in Guinness

Serves 4.

2 ounces/50 g flour

1 teaspoon salt

ground black pepper

1/2 teaspoon grated nutmeg

2 pounds/910 g chuck steak, cut into 1 inch/ 2 1/2 cm cubes

3 tablespoons oil

1 ounce/30 g butter

2 large onions, finely sliced

2 cloves garlic, crushed

1 teaspoon brown sugar

1 pint/470 ml Guinness

juice and zest of 1 orange

3 bay leaves

Preheat the oven to 350°F/180°C/Gas 4. Sift the flour into a shallow dish and stir in the salt, pepper and nutmeg. Coat the meat in the seasoned flour.

Heat half the oil and half the butter in a flameproof casserole. Add half the meat and fry for 2–3 minutes until evenly browned. Transfer to a plate, add the remaining oil and butter to the casserole and brown the remaining meat. Transfer to the plate.

Put the onions and garlic in the casserole and fry gently for 5 minutes, stirring constantly, then add the sugar. Cook over moderate heat for a further minute, stirring constantly, until the sugar caramelises.

Return the beef to the casserole and pour the Guinness over the top. Add the orange juice and half the zest together with 1 bay leaf and bring to a boil. Cover and cook for 1 1/2–2 hours, stirring occasionally, adding a little water to the casserole if the liquid becomes too thick.

When the meat is tender, discard the bay leaf and adjust the seasoning, adding a little more nutmeg if necessary. Sprinkle the remaining zest over the meat, garnish with bay leaves and serve.

Mummy's Braised Beef

Renee's Yum-Yum
Chilli Recipe

I am very partial to chilli, and this is undoubtedly the best chilli I have ever tasted. I discovered this recipe several years ago in Telluride, Colorado. It is great served with tacos or rice, or just used as a filling for baked potatoes.

2 onions, sliced

3 tablespoons oil

1 green bell pepper (optional), sliced

1 1/2 pounds/680 g ground turkey

chilli powder

1 can (14 ounces/400 g) crushed tomatoes
    or 1 can whole tomatoes (crush before
    adding)

1 can (14 ounces/400 g) red kidney beans
    (drain some of the liquid before using)

1 can (14 ounces/400 g) spicy red beans

2 teaspoons sugar

2 teaspoons balsamic vinegar

chilli peppers (optional), sliced

tortilla chips

grated Cheddar cheese (optional), for
    garnish

Sauté the onions in oil until soft. Add the green bell pepper, if used. Add the turkey and sauté until it is no longer pink and crumbles slightly. Add a sprinkle of chilli powder, then stir in tomatoes. Taste and add more chilli powder if necessary. Cook for a further 5 minutes on low heat and allow the flavours to flow through.

Add the beans and cook for 15 minutes. Add the sugar, vinegar and chilli peppers if used. Cook for 5–10 minutes more. Let it sit.

Serve over tortilla chips with Cheddar cheese on top or a bowl of rice with lashings of sour cream.

Grand Teton National Park, Wyoming, USA

Nita Morgan's Calf Liver and Bacon

Nita Morgan is the mother of a very good friend of mine, Deborah Morgan, and is one of the wisest women I know. Famous not only for her wonderful sayings such as "To the moon, Alice" and "Easy greasy you've got a long way to slide", she is also known for this dish which is my favourite recipe. To create a very special taste, make sure you add tomato ketchup at the end.

Serves 4.

1 calf's liver

4 rashers bacon, chopped roughly

plain flour, some of it seasoned with salt and pepper

1 tablespoon olive oil

GRAVY

2 tablespoons flour

2 tablespoons tomato sauce

1 1/2 cup water

salt and pepper

Soak the liver in salted cold water for approximately half an hour to clean it. Remove from water, remove membrane and cut into 1 1/4 inch/3 cm thick slices.

Gently cook the bacon in a large frying pan. Remove from the pan to a plate. Cover with kitchen paper and place in the oven on very low heat to keep warm.

Dry the liver and coat with seasoned flour. Place the olive oil in a frying pan, add the liver and turn gently to cook through and brown. Remove the liver from the pan and place in the oven with the bacon to keep warm.

GRAVY

Sprinkle 2 tablespoons of flour into the pan and blend with the liver drippings. Stir continuously until all residue from the pan has been absorbed and the flour is cooked. Add tomato sauce. Remove from the heat and gradually add 1 1/2 cups of water to the pan, stirring continuously. Bring to the boil, stirring all the while, and continue stirring for 2–3 minutes until the gravy thickens and becomes smooth, and the flour is cooked. Season with salt and pepper to taste.

Place the liver and bacon into the frying pan and mix with the gravy just before serving with mashed potatoes and garden peas.

Kidneys Turbigo

4–6 lamb's kidneys

4 ounces/110 g chipolata sausages

1 1/2 ounces/40 g butter

1 onion, chopped

2 ounces/50 g mushrooms, quartered

1 teaspoon sherry

1 teaspoon tomato purée

7 1/2 fl. ounces/220 ml stock

1 teaspoon plain flour

1 bay leaf

salt and pepper for seasoning

4 slices bread

chopped parsley and croutons, for garnish

Skin the kidneys, cut them into half and remove the core. Brown the kidneys, then the sausages in hot butter and remove to a dish.

Add the chopped onion and mushrooms to the pan. Season and cook for another 4–6 minutes. Add the sherry, tomato purée and stock. Add flour to thicken as required. Bring to the boil and add kidneys, sausages and bay leaf. Adjust the seasoning and simmer for 20 minutes.

Cut the bread into triangles. Place the bread on a dish, top with kidneys and sausages, dust with chopped parsley and serve surrounded with croutons.

Beef Wellington/
Boeuf St Jacques

fillet of beef (about 1 pound/450 g, serves
    2–3 people)

truffles (just a few)

slivers of garlic

salt and pepper to taste

brandy

slices of bread

goose liver pâté (I often use any kind
    available)

puff pastry (frozen will do)

beaten egg or milk

Cut slits into the fillet. Insert the truffles
and slivers of garlic. Season with salt and
pepper.

In a heavy pan, brown the fillet on
both sides (about 5 minutes each side),
turning with kitchen tongs.

Pour over about half a cup of brandy
and flame. Light the beef so the brandy
burns, and baste the meat in the juices.
Turn the fillet for another 5 minutes in
the juices.

Spread thick slices of bread (sufficient to
go under the fillet) with goose liver pâté.
Roll out the puff pastry according to
instructions on the package. Shortcrust
can also be used, or even filo if there is
no other. Many people prefer shortcrust.
The pastry should be big enough to
enclose the fillet entirely.

Put bread with pâté onto pastry, place
fillet on top of bread, close pastry around
fillet, crimping pastry closure along the
top. Brush with beaten egg or milk.

Bake in the oven at 400°F/200°C/Gas 6
for about 20 minutes or until pastry is
done and brown. The beef wellington
should be medium rare with this method,
but can sometimes be a bit on the rare
side, depending on how thick the fillet is.
If you get one of the thicker ones, cook it
for a bit longer before putting it into the
pastry shell.

I very often do this without the pastry,
just flaming the fillet in brandy. This is
Boeuf St Jacques.

Lamb Cutlets with
Pinenuts and Olives

Serves 4.

13^1/$_2$ fl. ounces/400 ml lamb stock

5 fl. ounces/150 ml red wine

3 cloves garlic, crushed

12 lamb cutlets

12 pitted kalamata olives

2 tomatoes, chopped

^{1}/$_2$ ounce/15 g pinenuts, toasted

2 tablespoons shredded basil

TO SERVE

mashed potatoes

seasonal vegetables

Place the stock, wine and garlic in a pan,
bring to the boil and bubble until the
liquid is reduced by about half.

Meanwhile, grill the lamb cutlets for
10–15 minutes, or until cooked to your
liking.

Lower the heat under the reduced sauce
and add the olives and tomatoes. Simmer
for 5 minutes until heated through.

To serve, place a spoonful of mashed
potato in the centre of each serving plate
and arrange the cutlets in front with the
vegetables of your choice behind. Spoon
over the sauce and sprinkle with the
pinenuts and basil.

Bernadette's Field Rabbit with Mustard Sauce

Rabbit is one of my favourite meat dishes, and this fabulous traditional French recipe kindly given to me by a lady who comes from France has become a well-loved recipe. When living in Scotland, I used to shoot rabbits on the farm and would spend time skinning and preparing them, which would make the meal worth all the effort.

1 large rabbit, cut into pieces

thyme

1 bay leaf

4 cloves garlic, crushed

rosemary

1 onion, sliced

Dijon mustard

bacon (same number of pieces as rabbit)

breadcrumbs

white wine

1 teaspoon wine vinegar

Chateau Chenonceau, Loire, France

Begin by placing the rabbit in an ovenproof earthenware dish with the thyme, bay leaf, garlic cloves, a little rosemary (too much will overwhelm the other flavours), and onion.

Discard the herbs and onion. Brush the rabbit pieces with mustard, crown each with a generous sprig of thyme and wrap in a piece of bacon.

Arrange the pieces in an oiled gratin dish, sprinkle a few breadcrumbs over each piece, and cook in a preheated oven at 375°F/190°C/Gas 5 for 30 minutes.

Deglaze the gratin dish with some white wine and wine vinegar and serve the rabbit, very hot, with baked potatoes and a green salad garnished with garlic croutons.

JC's Pork Roast

If there was ever a man who was a splendid cook, it is Jonathan Collins, my favourite trekking partner and old neighbour. I am honoured that he shared this recipe with me. The final result is sensational but it is important to find the right cut of pork and to cook it slowly, so it becomes tender and melts in the mouth. But beware – it is incredibly rich. Serve small helpings.

Serves 6-8.

1 pork butt (neck of the pig), around 3 pounds/1 ¹/₂ kg

salt

olive oil

fresh rosemary

6 medium cloves garlic

2-3 cans (13¹/₂ fl. ounces/400 ml) chicken stock

¹/₄ bottle white wine

Drain the meat if necessary, season it with salt, and massage liberal amounts of olive oil all over the meat.

Pluck the rosemary leaves, roughly chop them and then pound into a thick paste with the garlic, using a pestle and mortar. Add olive oil and keep pounding.

Spread the paste over the meat. It may not be possible to cover all the meat; cover as much as you can without having the paste fall off.

Leave the meat for 10 minutes to allow the paste to stick. Then pour more olive oil over the meat. Be generous.

To prepare the chicken stock, add ¹/₄ bottle of white wine with the chicken stock. Pour the stock into a deep baking tray and stand the meat in it. The stock needs to be at least ¹/₂ inch/1 cm in depth (around 25 fl. ounces/750 ml).

Cook in an oven between 325°F/170°C/Gas 3 and 350°F/180°C/Gas 4 for a minimum of 4 hours. Take the meat out and baste it with the stock every 20–30 minutes. You will need to top up the stock and white wine mixture to ensure the meat continues to cook in the juices. The meat will be ready any time after 4 hours. For best results, cook for 5¹/₂–6 hours, at which point the meat falls off the knife and melts in your mouth.

Serve with the jus and a simple gratin and salad.

Roast Pork Tenderloin with Sun-Dried Cranberry Stuffing

Serves 4–6.

1 pork tenderloin, about 1 1/2–2 pounds/
   680–910 g, butterflied, or two 1 pound/
   450 g tenderloins

1 cup water

3/4 cup sun-dried cranberries

2 tablespoons pinenuts, toasted

1 teaspoon ground cinnamon

pinch of ground cloves

2 tablespoons brown sugar

1–2 teaspoons chilli powder

salt and pepper

1/2 cup all-purpose flour, seasoned with salt
   and freshly ground pepper

2 tablespoons vegetable oil

Preheat the oven to 400°F/200°C/ Gas 6. Butterfly the pork tenderloin, if using only one.

Bring 1 cup of water to the boil in a medium saucepan. Add the cranberries, remove from heat and let rest for 1 hour. Drain, reserving the liquid, and place in the bowl of a food processor. Add the pinenuts, cinnamon, cloves, brown sugar, chilli powder and a few table-spoons of the liquid. Pulse until coarsely chopped, and remove to a bowl.

Place the tenderloin on a work surface and season both sides with salt and pepper. Spread a thin layer of the stuffing down the centre. Fold each side over the filling and tie with butcher's twine. Dredge lightly in flour.

Heat the oil in an ovenproof sauté pan. Sauté the tenderloin on all sides until golden brown. Place in the oven and roast until almost cooked through, about 10–14 minutes.

Remove and let it rest for 10 minutes before slicing into 1 inch/2 1/2 cm pieces.

SAUCE FOR PORK TENDERLOIN

2 tablespoons olive oil

1 small onion, finely chopped

1 carrot, finely diced

1 stalk celery, finely diced

2 cloves garlic, finely chopped

4 cups chicken stock

1/2 cup apple juice

1 teaspoon crushed chipotle chilli pepper

1 teaspoon black peppercorns

1 tablespoon butter

salt

Heat the oil in a medium saucepan over medium heat. Add the onion, carrot and celery and cook until soft, about 8–10 minutes. Add the garlic and cook for 2 minutes. Add the next four ingredients, increase heat to high and cook the sauce until reduced to 2 cups, about 10–12 minutes.

Strain the sauce into a small saucepan and bring to a simmer. Whisk in the butter and season with salt to taste.

Pour over the sliced pork and serve immediately.

Lamb with Pink-Eye Potato, Tomato and Spinach

Serves 4.

4 trim lamb eye of short loin

3 cloves garlic, crushed

1 sweet onion, chopped

10 egg tomatoes, skinned, seeded and chopped

2 sprigs thyme

2/3 fl. ounces/20 ml olive oil

1 bunch English spinach, stemmed

1 1/2 ounces/40 g butter, plus enough to deglaze pan

4 large pink-eye potatoes, boiled and peeled

1 fl. ounce/30 ml balsamic vinegar

3 fl. ounces/90 ml pinot noir

4 sprigs rosemary

salt and freshly ground black pepper

Sear the loins on all sides in hot oil. Set aside to rest.

Fry the garlic, onion, tomatoes and thyme in olive oil until just cooked. Season. Blanch the spinach, add butter and toss. Slice the potatoes and set aside.

To serve, place sliced potatoes in four 4 inch/10 cm rings and pour on vinegar. Spoon on a layer of tomato and onion and top with spinach. Slice the lamb and arrange on top of the spinach. Deglaze the pan with butter and wine and pour over the lamb.

Saddle of Lamb with Balsamic Vinegar

Serves 4.

2 pounds/910 g loin of lamb

salt and freshly ground black pepper

1 tablespoon parsley, finely chopped

1 tablespoon fresh chives, snipped

half a head of lettuce, shredded

tomatoes, or other seasonal vegetables, diced

FOR THE VINAIGRETTE

1 tablespoon balsamic vinegar

3 tablespoons olive oil

salt and pepper

Season the lamb with salt and freshly ground black pepper and sprinkle the herbs over. Roast at 400°F/200°C/Gas 6 for about 15–17 minutes, or until browned on the outside and rare in the centre. It is supposed to be pink. Remove from the oven and cool slightly.

For the vinaigrette, mix the balsamic vinegar and olive oil, and season with salt and pepper.

To serve, place shredded lettuce on plates. Slice the lamb thinly and arrange on lettuce. Drizzle the vinaigrette on top of the lamb. Decorate with diced tomatoes.

Lamb with Pink-Eye Potato, Tomato and Spinach

POULTRY

China

Granny Lee's Special Chicken Pie

One of the family's secret recipes that has been used for many years is Granny's Chicken Pie. It is a huge success at picnics or summer lunches. The key is in the making of the pastry, but once mastered, it will never be forgotten for its lightness and flavour.

FOR CHICKEN AND STOCK

1 good-sized chicken

1 onion, chopped

2–3 bay leaves

giblets

1 chicken stock cube

FOR THE FILLING

2/3 ounce/20 g butter

1 tablespoon cornflour

a few mushrooms, sliced

salt and pepper

FOR THE PASTRY

14 ounces/400 g self-raising flour (sometimes Granny used wholemeal flour)

8 ounces/225 g butter

salt

Put the chicken in a pot with the chopped onion, bay leaves, giblets and chicken stock cube. Add water to not quite cover the chicken. Simmer gently until cooked, about 30 minutes. Lift out the chicken. Strain stock and leave overnight. Remove the fat layer on top the next day. Take the chicken off bones.

Melt the butter and add cornflour mixed with the chicken stock. Add the chicken and mushrooms and cook down till the filling is just runny. Season to taste.

Place the flour on a working surface. Rub in the butter and a little salt. Knead and roll out the pastry. Line a pie dish with pastry and prick the dough with a fork. Add the chicken and mushroom filling. Cover with a layer of pastry, prick the top and crimp the edges together with a fork. Bake in the oven at 350°F/180°C/ Gas 4 until light brown.

Lyn Pooley's Chicken Coronation

This is another favourite recipe that reminds me of home. During the summer months Lyn would serve this regularly. Use this for a lunch in the garden on a lovely summer's day and complete it with new potatoes and salad.

Serves 6–8.

2 young roasting chickens
salt and pepper

CREAM OF CURRY SAUCE

1 tablespoon oil

2 ounces/50 g onion, finely chopped

1 dessertspoon curry powder

1 teaspoon tomato purée

1 wineglass red wine

1 glass water

bay leaf

salt and pepper

1 teaspoon sugar

lemon juice

3/4 pint/350 ml mayonnaise

1–2 tablespoons apricot purée

2–3 tablespoons whipped cream

paprika

Season the chickens and grill for 30 minutes in an oven at 180°C/350°F/ Gas 4. Once cooked, leave the chickens to cool, remove the skin and bones and collect the meat in a separate bowl.

TO PREPARE CREAM OF CURRY SAUCE

Heat the oil. Fry the onion, then add curry powder. Add the tomato purée, wine, 1 glass of water and bay leaf. Bring to the boil and add the salt and pepper, sugar and lemon juice. Simmer for 5–10 minutes. Strain and cool. When cool, add the mayonnaise and apricot purée to taste. Finish by folding in the whipped cream. Slowly stir the small pieces of chicken into the cream of curry sauce and sprinkle lightly with paprika for decoration and serve cold.

Marrakech, Morocco

Moroccan Tagine of Chicken with Pickled Lemon and Olives

An unusual recipe that I came across in Morocco. Cook the chicken slowly so that it is tender and ensure that the lemons are ripe and juicy to bring out the best flavour.

1 whole chicken

salt and vinegar (2 cups) for washing chicken

a few strands saffron soaked in $^1/_4$ cup of hot water

4 cloves garlic, crushed

2 onions, diced

2 ounces/50 g butter

1 pickled lemon, pulp and skin separated

1 teaspoon lemon juice

3 ounces/85 g olives

2 tablespoons olive oil

MARINADE

1 cup sunflower oil

salt and pepper seasoning

$^1/_2$ coffeespoon ginger

a few drops yellow colouring

Wash the chicken with a lot of salt and vinegar and rewash with running water. Soak the saffron threads in $^1/_4$ cup of hot water.

Mix the marinade ingredients. Marinate the chicken overnight.

The next day, place the chicken with its marinade in a large pot on the stove. Add the garlic, onions and butter and cook for 10 minutes. Add water to cover half the chicken and cook for another 25 minutes.

Add the saffron threads and the pulp of the pickled lemon. Five minutes before you take out the chicken, add lemon juice and the olives.

Remove the chicken from the sauce and set aside. Reduce the sauce until slightly thickened, then put the chicken back into the sauce and add olive oil.

Garnish the chicken with sliced skin of pickled lemon.

Mrs Chapman's Tandoori Chicken

4 chicken breasts

1 clove garlic, crushed

1–2 cartons yoghurt

Sharwoods Tandoori Paste

lemon juice

Twenty-four hours before you barbecue or bake your chicken breasts, marinate them in crushed garlic mixed with 1 or 2 cartons of yoghurt, depending on how many breasts you are using, a jar of Sharwoods Tandoori Paste or powder and a good dash of fresh lemon juice, then just cook normally.

Incidentally, I use virtually the same recipe for Chicken Tikka, exchanging Sharwoods Tandoori Paste with Sharwoods Tikka Paste, but cube your chicken before marinating, and serve on skewers.

Serve with a salad and jacket potatoes.

Moroccan Tagine of Chicken with Pickled Lemon and Olives

Dinner at Forter Castle, Scotland

Braised Pheasants in Cider with Caramelised Cox's Apples

Serves 4–6.

1 tablespoon butter

1 tablespoon oil

2 pheasants

salt and freshly milled black pepper

12 shallots

2 sprigs fresh thyme

1 bay leaf

3 tablespoons Calvados

1³/₄ pints/830 ml medium cider

1 heaped teaspoon flour and
    1 heaped teaspoon butter mixed
    to a paste

FOR THE CARAMELISED APPLES

1¹/₂ ounces/40 g butter, melted

3 medium Cox's apples, cored and cut
    into chunks with skin on

4 ounces/110 g granulated sugar

You'll need a flameproof casserole or saucepan, large enough for the pheasants to sit in comfortably.

In a heavy frying pan, heat the butter and oil together until quite hot, then brown the pheasants one by one in the hot fat until they're a good golden colour all over. Then place them side by side, with breasts uppermost, in the base of the casserole. Season them well with salt and pepper. Brown the shallots in the fat remaining in the frying pan and add the shallots to the pheasants along with the thyme and bay leaf.

Pour the Calvados into a ladle and gently rest the bowl of the ladle on a low gas flame or an electric hotplate – you need to get both the ladle and the Calvados nice and hot. Test it with your little finger, then ask someone to set a match to it while you hold it over the pheasants – or balance the ladle on the side of the casserole and do it yourself. When alight, pour the flaming Calvados all over the pheasant. The alcohol will burn off, leaving just the beautiful essence to flavour the birds. Now pour in the cider and bring everything up to a very gentle simmer. Put a tight lid on and let the pheasants braise slowly for 1–1¹/₄ hours or until they're tender.

When the pheasants are cooked, remove them and the shallots to a warmed serving plate and keep warm. Then boil the liquid in the casserole very briskly (without the lid) until it has reduced slightly. Then whisk in the flour and butter paste with a balloon whisk, which will slightly thicken it when it comes back to the boil. Carve the pheasants and serve with the shallots and the sauce poured over and garnished with the caramelised apples.

CARAMELISING THE APPLES

Towards the end of the cooking time, preheat the grill, line the grill pan with foil and brush it with the melted butter. Then brush each piece of apple with melted butter and dip it in sugar to coat it well all over. Arrange the apple sections on the buttered foil. When the grill is hot, grill them about 2 inches/5 cm away from the element for 6 minutes or until the sugar caramelises, then turn them over and caramelise the sugar on the other side. When they're done, they will keep warm without coming to any harm.

Saturday Market at Namche Bazaar, Nepal

TIBETAN HOSPITALITY

High in the Himalayas, in the autonomous region of southwest China bordering on India and Nepal, lies a land of natural beauty and culture – Tibet, the fabled Shangri-La or Lost Horizon. In this cold, hostile environment live Tibetan tribes such as my little friend Norgay's. They hold a respect for the elements that is rooted in an animistic doctrine predating Buddhism, the religion of the majority in Tibet. Norgay believes that every being has a soul.

The land being unsuited for agriculture, Norgay's family raises herds of yak for food. Tending his herd of yak on the green rolling hills, little Norgay sits dreaming, ignoring his friends who are looking after their own herds of the shaggy, ox-like animals. Yak produce milk and cheese for the Tibetans, and are their source of meat, leather and textiles. This animal has become a symbol of Tibet.

Suddenly Norgay's attention is caught by a cloud of dust erupting from the track road in the distance. "Visitors!" he shouts excitedly, pointing in the direction of a jeep moving slowly towards them. Visitors are a welcome diversion, for they bring news of the outside world.

Our jeep draws up outside the Tibetan house brightly painted with little pointed flags flying. Out we jump and remark that we are hungry and where can we eat? Norgay's mother answers promptly, "Why, here of course. We love visitors and will cook one of our meals for you to remember us by." Such unreserved hospitality is typical of the Tibetans.

We sit talking with the children and taking photos of the yak that have also wandered down to the village to see the excitement. Meanwhile Norgay's mother produces the largest frying pan I have ever seen and soon there is a delicious aroma – nothing on this earth smells or stimulates the gastric juices faster than hot sizzling onions. Then the potatoes are thrown in, followed by chopped yak meat and a fistful of Tibetan herbs. Soon we are sitting down to a wonderful meal, offered with much warmth and hospitality.

Sadly, we soon have to be on our way. Taking more photos and kissing the children, we say our goodbyes. Laughing, they climb onto the back of our jeep to delay our departure. It has been a wonderful day for Norgay. He knows he has to stay to guard the yak, but one day he will travel and be a visitor himself to another country, where hopefully he too will find warmth and hospitality.

Boned Chicken Curry

Serves 4.

1½ ounces/40 g lard

4 frying chicken joints

2 onions, peeled and chopped

1 ounce/30 g flour

1 tablespoon curry powder, more if desired

1 chicken stock cube dissolved in 1 cup
    water

1 tablespoon mango chutney

1 tablespoon blackcurrant jelly

salt and pepper

1 dessert apple

1 ounce/30 g sultanas

Melt 1 ounce/30 g lard in a fairly large
pan and fry the chicken joints on both
sides until golden brown. Take them
from the pan and carefully remove skin
and bones.

Melt the remaining lard in the pan and
fry the onions until they are soft. Blend
in the flour and curry powder and fry the
mixture for 1 minute. Add stock a little
at a time, then bring to boiling point and
simmer until sauce has thickened. Stir
in the mango chutney and blackcurrant
jelly. Season with salt and pepper.

Replace the chicken joints in the pan,
cover and simmer gently for 30 minutes
or until the chicken is tender. Meanwhile,
peel, core and chop the apple. Stir in the
sultanas and apple and cook for a further
5 minutes. Serve with boiled rice and
side dishes of fried poppadums, sliced
tomatoes or bell peppers, mango chutney
and peanuts.

Mrs Chapman's Tarragon Chicken

4 chicken breasts

1 Knorr Swiss garlic and herb stock cube

2 bay leaves

1 piece lemon peel

chives

Hellmans light mayonnaise

2 tablespoons cream

salt and freshly ground black pepper

parsley to garnish

Bring the water (just enough to cover
the chicken breasts) to the boil and add a
Knorr Swiss garlic and herb stock cube,
2 bay leaves and a piece of lemon peel.
Add the chicken breasts and simmer
very gently, making sure the meat is
covered at all times with the liquid and
turned regularly. They don't take long,
5 minutes will do, and you can check by
slitting open and peeping.

When cooked, remove from heat and
leave to cool in the liquid. Snip a lot of
chives into the liquid.

Meanwhile, mix enough Hellmans light
mayonnaise and a small amount of cream
(2 tablespoons) to cover the meat, and
you can thin it a bit with the cold liquid
the chicken was cooked in. Coat the
cold sliced chicken with the sauce, then
season with salt and freshly ground black
pepper. Garnish with parsley.

This can be served cold at a summer
picnic.

Chicken Crepes with Basil Mayonnaise

This is a recipe I only discovered recently but it is one I love. This makes a perfect lunch and is incredibly tasty.

1 egg

10 fl. ounces/300 ml milk

3/4 ounce/20 g butter, melted

2 teaspoons Dijon mustard

4 ounces/110 g all-purpose (plain) flour, sifted

4 chicken thigh fillets, trimmed

8 fl. ounces/240 ml strong chicken stock

2 teaspoons pickled pink peppercorns

4 fl. ounces/120 ml light (single) cream

2 tablespoons sun-dried tomatoes, sliced

2 teaspoons tomato paste (passato)

basil mayonnaise, for serving

Chicken Crepes with Basil Mayonnaise

Beat together the egg, milk, butter and mustard. Whisk the liquid into the flour until no lumps of flour remain. Cover and refrigerate for 30 minutes.

Place the chicken fillets in a shallow pan with the stock and peppercorns. Simmer for 5 minutes or until chicken is cooked, turning the fillets over occasionally. Turn the heat off and allow the fillets to rest in the stock for 5 minutes. Remove the chicken and slice thinly. Cook the stock over a high heat until reduced to almost nothing, then add the cream, tomatoes, tomato paste and chicken slices. Simmer over the lowest possible heat until required.

Heat a 6 inch/15 cm crepe or omelette pan over a medium heat. Add a little butter, then enough pancake batter to make a small crepe. Cook the pancakes until golden on both sides. Cover with foil and place in a warm oven until required. Fold the pancakes in half, place the chicken in the middle and serve with basil mayonnaise.

Honey-Glazed Duck Breast with Kumara and Ginger Ravioli

Serves 10.

10 duck breasts, trimmed and skin and fat scored

MARINADE

10 fl. ounces/300 ml soy sauce

1 tablespoon Dijon mustard

2 tablespoons honey

the roots from 1 bunch coriander, chopped finely

leaves from 1/2 bunch coriander

3 1/2 ounces/100 g ginger, chopped finely

4 cloves garlic, chopped finely

RAVIOLI

4 1/2 pounds/2 kg kumara

1 onion, chopped finely

1 clove garlic, chopped finely

2 tablespoons grated ginger

1 tablespoon butter

salt and freshly ground pepper

40 wonton wrappers

SAUCE

8 1/2 fl. ounces/250 ml duck stock

4 star anise, crushed

8 1/2 fl. ounces/250 ml veal demi-glace

TO SERVE

3 bunches baby bok choy, trimmed and steamed

1 pound/450 g beanettes or baby beans, topped, tailed and steamed

3 punnets shiitake mushrooms, sautéed in a little peanut oil with salt and pepper to taste

TO MARINATE DUCK BREASTS

Place duck breasts in a non-corrodible vessel. Combine all the marinade ingredients, pour over the duck, cover and refrigerate for at least 3 hours, turning several times.

TO MAKE KUMARA RAVIOLI

Wrap the whole kumara or kumara pieces in foil and roast in a 350°F/180°C/Gas 4 oven for about 45 minutes or until soft. Sauté the onion, garlic and ginger in butter until the onion is soft. Scoop out the flesh from the kumara, purée in a food processor, then mix with the onion/ginger mixture and season with salt and pepper.

Spread out half of the wonton wrappers on a flat surface, brush with water and spoon 2 teaspoonfuls of the kumara mixture in the centre of each wrapper. Cover with the remaining wonton wrappers, cut with a round biscuit cutter and press the edges together to seal. Cover the ravioli with a slightly dampened tea towel and set aside until ready to cook.

TO MAKE THE SAUCE

Simmer the duck stock with the star anise until the stock is anise-flavoured. Strain, discard the solids and place the stock in a saucepan with the veal demi-glace. Cook over low heat until the sauce boils. Set aside in a warm place.

TO COOK THE DUCK AND RAVIOLI

Remove duck breasts from the marinade. Drain and then grill for 4 minutes on each side or until cooked and the skin is crisp.

While the duck is cooking, bring a saucepan of salted water to the boil, reduce the heat and drop in the ravioli. Cook until the pasta is tender, then remove the ravioli with a slotted spoon to a colander to drain. Pour over a little melted butter just before serving.

TO SERVE

Spoon some sauce on each heated serving plate and pile some of the cooked vegetables in the centre. Slice the duck breasts and arrange on the vegetables. Serve at once with two of the ravioli to one side.

Eva Owies' Lemon Chicken

When I first arrived in Hong Kong, I spent many Saturdays discovering new recipes. I was asked by Paul, my boyfriend at the time, to cook his favourite recipe which was created by his mother, of whom I am very fond. This has remained one of my best-loved chicken dishes. It is quick to cook and makes a wonderful meal.

4 chicken drumsticks

flour seasoned with salt, pepper and paprika

1–2 ounces/30–50 g butter

1/2 cup lemon juice

1/4 cup olive oil

1 tablespoon oyster sauce

Roll the chicken drumsticks in plain flour seasoned with salt, pepper and paprika. Put them in an ovenproof dish with butter, then bake in a 350°F/180°C/Gas 4 oven for 30 minutes. Take out of the oven and turn. Beat lemon juice, olive oil and oyster sauce together with a fork and pour the mixture over the chicken. Bake for another 30 minutes. Serve with a crisp green salad.

Mrs Nicholas' Chicken Special

This is a recipe that I never get tired of. I had just returned from travelling in South America for a year with a dear friend, Dan Nicholas. It was Boxing Day and we visited his parents in Shropshire. Mrs Nicholas created this amazing dish with the leftover turkey pieces. I often cook this recipe after Christmas but sometimes during the year I replace the turkey with chicken pieces.

2 slices bacon or turkey (leftovers will do)

sliced breast of chicken, precooked

peas, broccoli or sweetcorn, preboiled

2 cans Campbell's Chicken Soup

1 cup mayonnaise

1 teaspoon lemon juice

1 teaspoon curry powder

1/2 cup grated cheese

1/2 cup plain crisps/potato chips

Fry the bacon until crisp. Place the chicken, bacon and vegetables in an ovenproof dish. Combine the soup, mayonnaise, lemon juice and curry powder in a bowl and pour over the chicken and vegetables. Sprinkle cheese on top and crumbled crisps. Cook in a 350°F/180°C/Gas 4 oven for 25 minutes.

Soy Sauce and Honey Marinated Chicken

4 chicken breasts

1/2 cup soy sauce

2 tablespoons honey

3–4 stalks spring onions

2 cloves garlic, chopped

1 medium slice ginger, chopped

1/2 teaspoon five-spice powder

1/2 cup vegetable oil

1 tablespoon walnut oil

1/2 cup port

Combine all the ingredients except the chicken. Marinate the chicken and refrigerate for at least 4 hours. Bake for about 25 minutes in a 350°F/180°F/Gas 4 oven.

Bangkok Chicken and Rice

Bangkok Chicken and Rice

1 small boiling chicken, approximately 3$^1/_2$ pounds/1$^1/_2$ kg

1 pound/450 g onions, one onion left whole, the rest sliced thinly

1 bay leaf

1 sprig parsley

salt and freshly ground black pepper

1 pound/450 g long grain rice

3 tablespoons olive or vegetable oil

2 level tablespoons peanut butter

$^1/_2$ level teaspoon chilli powder

4 ounces/110 g peeled prawns

4 ounces/110 g diced cooked ham

1 level teaspoon cumin seeds

1$^1/_2$ level teaspoons coriander seeds

1 clove garlic

pinch of ground mace

half a cucumber, unpeeled, sliced thinly

2 hardboiled eggs, in wedges

8–12 large unpeeled cooked prawns

Put the chicken in a large pan with one whole peeled onion, the bay leaf and a sprig of parsley. Add salt and pepper and enough cold water to cover chicken. Bring to the boil, remove any scum from the surface, then cover the pan with a lid and simmer over gentle heat for about 2 hours or until chicken is tender.

Lift out the chicken and leave to cool slightly. Strain the stock through a fine sieve and use it to cook the rice until just tender. Drain the rice through a colander and cover it with a dry cloth. Remove skin from the chicken and cut the meat into small pieces.

Heat the oil in a large pan and fry the sliced onions over low heat until they begin to change colour. Stir in the peanut butter and chilli powder. Add the peeled prawns, diced ham and the chicken, and finally the rice, which should now be dry and fluffy. Continue frying over low heat, stirring frequently until the rice is slightly brown. Crush the cumin and coriander seeds and the garlic and stir them, with the mace, into the rice. Season to taste with salt.

Pile the rice and chicken mixture on to a serving plate and garnish with thin slices of cucumber, wedges of hardboiled egg and large prawns.

Arrange a number of small side dishes or bowls around the chicken. A suitable selection might include apricot and mango chutney, sliced tomatoes dressed with sugar and lemon juice, peeled and sliced oranges, and sliced green and red bell peppers with raw onion rings, both in a vinaigrette sauce. Other bowls could contain small wedges of fresh pineapple, sweetened with icing sugar, fried sliced bananas with lemon juice, and fresh shredded toasted coconut. Shelled almonds or cashew nuts fried in a little butter are also frequently served.

Roast Garlic Goose with Braised Red Cabbage

FOR THE GOOSE

11–12 pounds/5–5$\frac{1}{2}$ kg goose, giblets removed

1 small bunch fresh thyme

1 unwaxed lemon, quartered

2 heads garlic, cloves broken apart but left unpeeled

salt and freshly ground black pepper

2 tablespoons flour

3$\frac{1}{3}$ fl. ounces/100 ml white wine

1$\frac{1}{4}$ pints/600 ml chicken or giblet stock

FOR THE BRAISED RED CABBAGE

3 pounds/1$\frac{1}{3}$ kg red cabbage, sliced coarsely

2 red onions, sliced

4 ounces/110 g sultanas

1 teaspoon caraway seeds

4 tablespoons red wine vinegar

2 teaspoons Bovril

1 tablespoon Oxo gravy granules

4 tablespoons soft brown sugar

salt and pepper

1$\frac{1}{2}$ ounces/40 g butter

TO COOK GOOSE

Place the goose on a wire rack in a large roasting tin. Stuff the neck cavity with the thyme and lemon and half the cloves of garlic. Place the remaining cloves of garlic around the goose in the bottom of the roasting pan. Season with plenty of salt and pepper and prick the skin with a fork.

Place the goose in an oven preheated to 425°F/220°C/Gas 7 and roast the goose for 30 minutes. Baste the goose with the fat in the tin. Turn down the heat to 350°F/180°C/Gas 4 and roast for a further 1$\frac{1}{2}$–2 hours. Keep basting at least every half hour; you will probably need to pour off the copious quantities of fat from the roasting tin. To see if the goose is cooked, insert a skewer into the legs and check that the juices run clear. Remove the goose to a serving dish and keep warm.

Pour off all but 2 tablespoons fat from the roasting tin. Stir flour into the fat in the roasting tin and cook on top of the stove for 1–2 minutes, squashing the softened garlic cloves out of their skins as you stir. Add the white wine and whisk until thickened. Bubble for 3–4 minutes. Stir in the chicken or giblet stock and cook for a further 5 minutes. Season with salt and pepper. Strain gravy through a fine sieve, and serve with the carved goose and braised red cabbage.

TO BRAISE RED CABBAGE

In a casserole, layer the cabbage with onion slices, sultanas, caraway seeds, red wine vinegar, Bovril, gravy granules and soft brown sugar. Season well with salt and pepper and dot with butter. Cover and place in an oven preheated to 325°F/170°C/Gas 3 for 2$\frac{1}{2}$ hours, stirring halfway through cooking.

Roast Garlic Goose with Braised Red Cabbage

Petra, Jordan

Grilled Salt and Pepper Quail

Serves 4 as a starter, 2 as a main course.

4 quails

1 teaspoon Sichuan peppercorns

1 teaspoon black peppercorns

1 teaspoon Maldon salt

1 tablespoon olive oil

1 tablespoon lemon juice

2 tablespoons light soy sauce

1–2 organic lemons, halved

1 tablespoon honey

Grilled Salt and Pepper Quail

There are various ways to treat the quail. Either leave them whole, or cut them in half along the back and breastbone using kitchen shears, or you can spatchcock them, which means cutting out the backbone with kitchen shears, then flattening the birds with your hand. If you are spatchcocking, skewer the birds with two skewers to keep them flat to the grill.

Place the quail in a grill-proof dish. Coarsely crush the peppercorns and half the salt and combine with the olive oil, lemon juice and 1 tablespoon light soy sauce. Rub this mixture all over the quail. Add the lemon halves to the quail. Leave to marinate in the fridge for at least 1 hour, then stand at room temperature for 30 minutes before cooking.

Remove the lemons and set aside. Heat the grill. With the halved or spatchcocked quail, cook them first for 5 minutes skin side down, then turn them skin side up for a further 5 minutes. With whole quail, give them 4 minutes for each breast and back. Mix the remaining soy sauce with the honey. Add the lemons to the quail, cut sides upwards, then brush the honey mixture over the skin of the quail and sprinkle with the remaining

salt. Grill for another 4–5 minutes, until both quail and lemons are well browned, adjusting the heat so the honey glaze doesn't scorch.

Test for readiness by pulling a leg. It shouldn't look red inside, but slightly pink is fine. Cover loosely with foil and leave to stand for 4–5 minutes before serving. Allow a lemon half per person to squeeze over the quail.

VEGETABLES

Thailand

Laos

LOVELY LAOS

You could easily miss Laos if you weren't looking for it. Nestled between Vietnam and Thailand, it lies off the beaten track. Transportation and other essential infrastructure are limited, discouraging tourists from including Laos in their travel plans. The country has also seen much fighting. This former French protectorate gained independence in 1953, and became a republic when the communist Pathet Lao overthrew the centuries-old monarchy some twenty years later. Compared to their neighbours, the Laotians are very poor and have a life expectancy of only 55 years.

My first impression was of an absence of hustle and bustle. The Laotians seem gentler and quieter than most people, and their way of life far more relaxed. Most of them live off the land. Wandering around, I was lucky to stumble upon a silk farm tucked away in the countryside, run by one of Laos' most famous women, Carol Cassidy. This remarkable American arrived in 1989, and set up Lao Textiles in the capital, Vientiane, manufacturing top quality silk products with original designs. Since she employs locals in this cottage industry, not only do her beautiful shawls and scarves have a uniquely Laotian feel, but many Laotian families have also been able to improve their standard of living.

Carol was kind enough to show me her silkworms. These unassuming little creatures feed on mulberry leaves, and they are the real creators of the silk so prized by us humans. It was quite amazing to see the silk being spun by the worms. The silk products, including an extensive array of picture collages and tapestries, are mostly for export. There are customers who ask Carol to make special items such as flags or national emblems. I did manage to pack a few things into my own travel bag!

When touring Southeast Asia, do not leave out Laos. You could get quite a bit from this underrated country! And you should certainly travel to the countryside to see those happy little silkworms magically transforming mulberry leaves into silk.

Aubergine Omelette

Patience is required when frying the omelette to make sure it doesn't break up, but it is well worth it. I have been cooking this for many years and it serves well with a salad in the summer.

Serves 8.

10³/₄ ounces/300 g aubergine

2 cloves garlic, finely chopped

8 large eggs

4 tablespoons sour cream

1 level teaspoon cumin

salt and freshly ground black pepper

2 ounces/50 g butter

12 medium-sized, flavoursome tomatoes

olive oil

a little castor sugar

flat-leaf parsley and Parmesan cheese, to garnish

Peel the aubergine and cut into dice about the size of croutons. Steam until tender, about 4–6 minutes. If you don't have a steamer, you can do this in a colander, covered with a lid, over a saucepan of boiling water.

Peel and finely chop the garlic. Beat the eggs with the sour cream and cumin. Season well with salt and pepper. In the omelette pan, fry the garlic gently in the butter to soften (but not brown). Add the steamed aubergine and fry briefly, tossing in the butter. Add the eggs. Make the omelette as normal, lifting the edges and tilting the pan to make sure the aubergine is evenly distributed. When the bottom is done, put the pan under a hot grill for a minute or two to set the top. Slide on to a flat plate and leave to cool.

Meanwhile, line a baking sheet with foil. Cut the tomatoes horizontally into slices about ¹/₄ inch/¹/₂ cm thick (discard those end slivers with too much skin). Brush oil on both sides and place in a single layer on the baking sheet. Sprinkle fairly generously with castor sugar and salt. Bake in a cool oven (300°F/150°F/Gas 2) for 25–30 minutes, then put under a hot grill for a minute to finish. Allow to cool, then distribute over the omelette. Sprinkle with chopped parsley and grated Parmesan cheese.

Nanna Poo's Yorkshire Pudding

I included this recipe in the vegetable section quite simply because it gets served with vegetables. My grandmother was a wonderful cook and apart from her gorgeous jam tarts, her Yorkshire Puddings are ones that I will always remember.

4 ounces/110 g flour

pinch of salt

1 egg, beaten

8 fl. ounces/240 ml milk

Mix the flour and salt together. Add the beaten egg, then pour in the milk. Beat until there are no lumps or air pockets.

Pre-warm the pudding tins and brush with a little grease. Add the batter and cook for 10 minutes at 400°F/200°C/Gas 6.

Serve with roast beef and roast potatoes.

Zucchini Frittata

Serves 2–4.

extra virgin olive oil

butter

1 small red onion, halved and sliced

2 zucchini, sliced diagonally $1/10$ inch/2.5 mm thick

6 large eggs

3 tablespoons freshly grated Pecorino cheese

$1/2$ bunch chives, chopped in $1 1/4$ inch/3 cm lengths

sea salt and freshly ground pepper

Preheat the oven to 350°F/180°C/Gas 4. Heat a little olive oil and butter in a 8 inch/20 cm heavy-based frying pan and stir-fry the onion over low heat until caramelised. Set aside in a bowl. Add a little more oil and butter to the pan and fry the zucchini on both sides until softened, then set aside with the onion.

Lightly whisk the eggs, Pecorino and chives in a bowl. Season, then stir in the onion and zucchini. Melt a little butter over high heat and add oil, then, when the butter foams, tip in the egg mixture. Reduce the heat and, with a wooden spatula, gradually draw the mixture from the pan's edge to the centre, forming large curds and distributing the ingredients evenly. Cook over low heat until almost set.

Transfer the pan to the preheated oven and cook until the frittata is just set. Remove from the oven and slip the frittata onto a warmed serving plate. Serve it in wedges with crusty sourdough bread and a rocket salad with toasted pinenuts.

Kilimanjaro, Africa

Jane Normanton's Roasted Red Pepper Rolls with Goat's Cheese

Serves 4.

6 medium red bell peppers

$1/2$ cup good olive oil

6 ounces/170 g mild goat cheese, no rind

12 bay leaves

De-seed the bell peppers and halve lengthwise. Brush lightly with a small amount of olive oil and place them on a baking sheet. Grill until the skins are charred. Put in a polythene bag, cool, then peel.

Cut the goat cheese into 12 pieces. Put a piece of cheese onto each bell pepper half and roll up.

Put the pepper rolls into a shallow baking dish and tuck a bay leaf between each roll. Add the rest of the olive oil. Cover with tin foil and bake in a 350°F/ 180°C/Gas 4 oven for 30–40 minutes.

Creamed Fresh Corn

Serves 4.

2 tablespoons olive oil

1 jalapeño pepper, seeded and diced

8 ears fresh corn, husks and silk removed, kernels cut from cobs

$1/4$ cup heavy cream

$1 1/4$ cups milk

$3/4$ teaspoon coarse salt

$1/4$ teaspoon freshly ground pepper

Heat the oil in a large sauté pan over medium heat. Add the jalapeño and cook for 1 minute. Add the corn; cook, stirring, until the kernels are tender but not browned, about 5 minutes. Remove from heat.

Transfer $1 1/2$ cups cooked corn to the bowl of a food processor fitted with a metal blade, and add the cream and milk. Process until the mixture is very smooth, about 3 minutes. Pass the mixture through a fine sieve into a medium bowl, pressing down on the solids to extract as much liquid as possible.

Return the strained liquid to the sauté pan, and stir to combine with remaining corn mixture. Cook over medium heat until the liquid just comes to a simmer. Remove from heat, and season with salt and pepper. Serve hot.

Lentils with Fresh Herbs

Serves 6.

8 ounces/225 g lentils

1/2 bulb garlic, separated into cloves, peeled and cut horizontally

3 tablespoons extra virgin olive oil

juice of 1 lemon

2–3 tablespoons chopped herbs (oregano, basil, summer savory, mint or marjoram)

sea salt and freshly ground black pepper

Cover the lentils with plenty of cold water, then add the garlic and bring to the boil. Simmer for about 20 minutes or until lentils are cooked. Drain, discarding the garlic, and toss with olive oil and lemon juice. Stir in the herbs and season. Serve warm.

Dhal (Spiced Lentils)

8 ounces/225 g lentils

2 tablespoons ghee or oil

1 onion, sliced or chopped

1 clove garlic, crushed

1 green or red chilli, chopped

1 1/2 teaspoons chilli powder (cayenne pepper)

3 cups water

8 fl. ounces/240 ml coconut milk

1 teaspoon salt

Wash and drain the lentils. Heat the ghee in a pan and stir-fry the onion and garlic for 2–3 minutes. Add the chopped chilli and stir-fry for 2 minutes. Add the chilli powder and lentils, then add water and bring to the boil, stirring occasionally. Reduce the heat to low and simmer for approximately 30 minutes. Add the coconut milk and salt and continue to cook for a further 10 minutes.

Kathmandu, Nepal

Spiced Potatoes with Cauliflower

3 tablespoons ghee

1 pound/450 g potatoes, peeled and cut into pieces

1 large onion, sliced or chopped

2 cloves garlic, chopped

$1/4$ teaspoon chilli powder

$1/2$ teaspoon turmeric

1 teaspoon coriander

1 teaspoon cumin

1 teaspoon salt

8 fl. ounces/240 ml weak coconut milk

1 pound/450 g cauliflower, cut into florets

4 fl. ounces/120 ml thick coconut milk

Melt the ghee in a pan. Add the potatoes and fry gently for 2–3 minutes. Add the onion and garlic to the pan and fry for a further 2–3 minutes. Add the spices and salt, stir, then add weak coconut milk. Bring to the boil and simmer for 10 minutes. Add the cauliflower and the thick coconut milk and cook till the vegetables are tender.

Simple Dali Cauliflower

Serves 4, as part of a rice meal.

1 medium head cauliflower

salt

2 tablespoons peanut or vegetable oil

2 teaspoons minced garlic, or 3–4 whole cloves garlic, smashed

Put a large pot of water on to boil. Meanwhile, remove and discard the leaves and core of the cauliflower. Cut the cauliflower into florets.

Once the water is boiling, add about 1 tablespoon salt, bring back to the boil, and toss in the cauliflower florets. Use a long-handled spoon to stir gently as the water comes back to the boil. Boil for about 1 minute, or until cauliflower is tender but still firm. Drain and set aside.

Heat a large wok over high heat. Add the oil and swirl to coat the wok. Toss in the garlic and stir-fry until it starts to turn golden, 15–20 seconds. Toss in the cauliflower and stir-fry for 30 seconds to 1 minute, pressing it against the side of the wok to sear it, but being careful not to mash it. Add $1/2$ teaspoon salt, stir-fry briefly, turn out onto a colourful plate, and serve. If using whole garlic, scatter them over the cauliflower.

The Best Eggplant Dish Ever

This recipe serves 4, as part of a rice meal.

3 dried Thai red chillies, soaked in warm water for 15 minutes to soften

1/4 cup finely chopped shallots

5 cloves garlic, minced

1 heaped tablespoon dried shrimp

1 teaspoon salt

1 medium tomato, coarsely chopped

2 tablespoons vegetable oil

1/4 cup (2 ounces/50 g) ground pork (optional)

1/2 teaspoon ground turmeric (optional)

4–5 medium eggplants (about 1 1/2 pounds/ 680 g), cut into 1/4 inch slices

5–8 leaves mint or coriander, coarsely torn

Bali

Drain the chillies and reserve the water. Chop them coarsely, discarding the tough stems, and place in a mortar or blender together with the shallots, garlic, dried shrimp and salt. Pound or process to a paste. If using the blender, you will probably need to add some of the water used to soak the chillies. Add the tomato and pound or blend briefly, then transfer the spice paste to a bowl and set aside.

Place a heavy pot with a tight-fitting lid over high heat. Add the oil and swirl to coat the bottom of the pot. Add the pork, if using, and brown briefly, then add the spice paste and optional turmeric. Lower heat to medium and cook, stirring, until aromatic, about 2 minutes. Add the eggplant slices and stir briefly, cover tightly, and reduce heat to low. Do not add water.

Cook for 45 minutes to 1 hour or until the eggplant is very tender and shapeless, checking every 5 minutes or so to ensure that nothing is sticking and to give the ingredients a brief stir. The dish can be prepared ahead to this point and then reheated; refrigerate if making more than 1 hour in advance.

Turn out into a shallow bowl and top with the mint or coriander. Serve warm or at room temperature.

The Best Eggplant Dish Ever

SALADS

China

Moscow, Russia

"Don't go!" advised the British Embassy in Beijing. Trouble was brewing in Moscow, but if we didn't make it soon, the borders would be sealed. My mother and I were to travel on the Trans-Siberian Express, from China through Mongolia up to the Russian border, then transfer to the Orient Express at Moscow for St Petersburg.

"Take all your food and water," we were told, so armed with a week's supply, we joined the crowds at Beijing Central Station. Our load was so heavy, we piled it onto a blanket – only to find that dragging a load can be a weighty task when you come to flights of steps! Locating our departure platform was a concern as nobody spoke English. We joined the longest queue. We were lucky.

"Leave your compartment securely locked all the time," said our well-wishers. Our first-class compartment looked like everyone else's and the train was packed to capacity, with passengers filling the corridors. The first night, we nervously locked ourselves in.

Our choices in the food car were limited to beetroot soup and black goulash laced with vodka. The cooks started early on the vodka and by lunchtime quite a party was in swing! In the next compartment we met British Embassy staff en route to Ulan Bator, the capital of Mongolia. They were well-equipped with happy hour gin and tonics. We joined them, adding our cheese and biscuits.

During the train's two-minute stops, Chinese merchants on board sold suede and leather jackets through the windows. This was how they made their living, and everyone benefited, including the Mongolians and Russians who could not get commodities. We jumped out to buy fresh food. The locals held out pieces of chicken, sometimes just one tomato or a bread roll to sell. It was all they had. Life was certainly tough here.

At the Russian border, the railway gauge changed, which meant the train had to be hoisted by crane and placed on different size bogies. This took 14 hours, giving us the opportunity to look around the border town. Although it was only September, the weather changed dramatically. When we left Beijing, we were wearing silk. Halfway through Siberia we were cold even in four layers of clothes. To keep warm, we made soup using the coal fire stove on board.

We were relieved to arrive in Moscow, though sad to leave our little nest of nearly a week. We were also surprised to see holes in the window of our compartment. We never did learn whether they were made by small stones as we sped by, or by bullets! But we were intact and on our way to St Petersburg in a gold and velvet Victorian-style tailcar. The following week fighting broke out in Moscow. By then we were home with our photographs and memories of a momentous train journey.

Chicken and Mango Summer Salad

While out lunching with my friend Deborah in Perth at a small café, we discovered this delicious salad. Not for the health-conscious as it does contain mayonnaise, but it is a wonderful summer salad with mangoes and strawberries.

MIX TOGETHER

4 chicken breasts, sliced

7 ounces/200 g snow peas

5 ounces/140 g snow pea sprouts

3 fresh mangoes (or tinned mango), sliced

1 red bell pepper, sliced finely

1 punnet strawberries, washed and sliced

salt and fresh ground black pepper

HOMEMADE MAYONNAISE

4 whole eggs

1 tablespoon Dijon mustard

1 tablespoon honey

salt and pepper

vegetable oil

white vinegar

1 mango

Prepare the dressing by blending together eggs, mustard, honey and seasoning. Add vegetable oil with the processor turning until the mixture is thick, then add a splash of white vinegar.

Blend the mayonnaise with an additional mango and toss through the salad.

Thinly slice all the vegetables, fruit and chicken. Put in a salad bowl and mix together gently. Pour over the mayonnaise dressing and fold in gently. This is a perfect salad either for a light lunch or as a refreshing small salad between courses at a large dinner party.

Caesar Salad

1 head lettuce

1 egg

2 cloves garlic, minced

3 tablespoons lemon juice

1/2 cup olive oil

4 anchovy fillets, drained and chopped

2 hardboiled eggs, in wedges

1/2 cup freshly grated cheese

3/4 cup croutons

CROUTONS

3 tablespoons unsalted butter

3 tablespoons mild olive oil

3 cups bread cubes

2 cloves garlic

1 teaspoon mixed salad herbs

3 tablespoons grated Parmesan cheese

Rinse the lettuce, dry and refrigerate, wrapped in a paper towel.

Whisk the egg, garlic, lemon juice and olive oil together and pour into the bottom of a salad bowl. Add the lettuce, anchovy and hardboiled eggs and toss with the dressing. Add the cheese and toss again. Sprinkle with croutons and serve immediately.

To make the croutons, heat the butter and oil over medium-high heat, add the bread and toss constantly for 3–4 minutes. Add garlic and herbs and cook until golden brown, for 25 minutes. Remove to a bowl and toss it with Parmesan cheese. Store in an airtight container until ready to use.

Farro Salad with Thinly Sliced Zucchini, Pinenuts and Lemon Zest

Serves 8–10.

12 ounces/340 g farro

coarse salt

1 small shallot, minced

grated zest and juice of 1¹/₂ lemons

3 tablespoons extra virgin olive oil

¹/₂ cup pinenuts

1 pound/450 g zucchini, ends trimmed

¹/₂ cup, loosely packed, fresh flat-leaf parsley
    leaves, roughly chopped

freshly ground pepper

4 ounces/110 g Parmesan-Reggiano cheese

Place the farro in a large saucepan, and add enough cold water to cover by about 3 inches/7¹/₂ cm. Bring to the boil over high heat. Add the salt and stir once. Reduce the heat to medium, and simmer until farro is *al dente* according to package instructions, about 10–12 minutes. Drain, and let cool.

In a small bowl, combine the shallot with lemon juice and salt. Let stand 15 minutes. Meanwhile, in a sauté pan, heat oil over medium heat, and add pinenuts. Cook, stirring until they are lightly toasted, about 5 minutes. Remove from heat, and add lemon zest to the pinenuts.

Using a mandoline or sharp knife, slice the zucchini crosswise as thin as possible, and place in a large bowl. Add the farro, pinenut mixture and parsley. Stir to combine. Stir in the shallot mixture and season with salt and pepper. Transfer to a large serving bowl.

Using a vegetable peeler, shave half the cheese over the salad. Toss to combine. This salad can be stored up to 6 hours in the refrigerator, covered with plastic wrap. Just before serving, shave remaining cheese on top.

Egypt

Madeline Pulling's Chinese Salad

I love Asian food and Madeline has perfected the art of Asian cooking. I first tasted this salad at a dinner party at her house in Hong Kong. It is important not to let the noodles become soggy so the salad remains nice and crunchy.

combined greens, iceberg and romaine lettuce (it must be a crunchy variety of lettuce to go with the noodles)

carrots, cut into julienne strips

scallions, sliced (use the ends so the salad doesn't get mushy)

coriander leaves

fresh noodles, preferably egg noodles from the wet market

DRESSING

1 cup hoisin sauce (from any Chinese food store)

2 tablespoons vinegar (apple cider is good)

1 tablespoon freshly grated ginger

2 tablespoons sesame oil

1 tablespoon Dijon mustard, if the hoisin you have is too sweet

1 tablespoon chilli sauce, depending how spicy you want it (we like it spicy, even in salads!)

$1/3$ cup olive oil, as a general binder

Wash the lettuce leaves well and prepare the other salad ingredients. Deep-fry the noodles.

Process all the dressing ingredients in a blender. Pour over the noodles and toss well just before serving, or the noodles will be soggy. Pour the noodles and dressing into a bowl with the prepared lettuce and serve immediately.

Lentil Salad with Tarragon, Shallots and Beets

Serves 8–10.

$3^1/2$ pounds/$1^1/2$ kg beets, trimmed

2 tablespoons plus $1/4$ cup extra virgin olive oil

$3^1/2$ teaspoons coarse salt, plus more for seasoning

$1/4$ cup water, plus more for cooking lentils

1 pound/450 g French green lentils, picked over

2 cloves garlic

2 dried bay leaves

1 shallot, minced

1 teaspoon Dijon mustard

2 tablespoons plus 1 teaspoon balsamic vinegar

1 tablespoon chopped fresh tarragon

freshly ground pepper

Preheat the oven to 350°C/180°F/Gas 4. In a medium bowl, toss the beets with 2 tablespoons oil and $1^1/2$ teaspoons salt. Arrange on a rimmed baking sheet, and pour $1/4$ cup water into the pan. Roast until the beets are easily pierced with the tip of a knife, 45 to 60 minutes. Remove from the oven and let cool. Peel and cut into $1/2$ inch cubes.

Meanwhile, combine the lentils, garlic and bay leaves in a saucepan. Add enough cold water to cover by about 3 inches/$7^1/2$ cm. Bring to the boil over medium-high heat, then reduce heat to medium-low. Simmer, stirring occasionally, until the lentils are tender but not mushy, 10–20 minutes. Stir in the remaining 2 teaspoons salt and cook about 5 minutes more. Drain in a colander and let cool.

Now, make a vinaigrette. In a small bowl, combine the shallot, mustard and vinegar; let stand 15 minutes. Slowly whisk in remaining $1/4$ cup oil in a steady stream.

Transfer the lentils to a large serving bowl. Pour the vinaigrette over the lentils, and add the tarragon. Toss well to combine. Toss in the beets. Season with salt and pepper and serve. If you are preparing ahead, cover with plastic wrap and refrigerate for up to 4 hours. Bring to room temperature before serving.

Janet Shafran's Wheat Berry and Barley Salad with Smoked Mozzarella

This filling recipe was given to me by a dear friend Janet, who was living in Singapore at the time. I have fond memories of this recipe as I shared it with another girlfriend, Mim, when visiting her house in Melbourne. I took one spoonful and was horrified by the terrible taste. We finally discovered the problem: Mim had substituted the cherry tomatoes with glazed cherries! It makes all the difference so please remember to use fresh cherry tomatoes!

Serves 6 as an entrée, or 8-10 as a side dish.

1 cup wheat berries (available in natural food stores)

1 cup pearl barley

1 small red onion, chopped fine

2 cloves garlic, minced and mashed to a paste with $1/2$ teaspoon salt

$1/4$ cup balsamic vinegar

$1/4$ cup olive oil, preferably extra virgin

6 scallions, chopped fine

$1 1/2$ cups cooked corn (cut from 2 large ears)

$1/2$ pound/225 g smoked Mozzarella cheese, diced fine

2 cups vine-ripened cherry tomatoes, halved

$1/2$ cup chopped fresh chives

salt and pepper seasoning

Into a pot of salted boiling water, stir wheat berries and cook at a slow boil for 30 minutes. Stir in the barley and cook grains at a slow boil for 40 minutes.

While the grains are cooking, in a large bowl, stir together the onion, garlic paste, vinegar and oil.

Drain the grains well and add them to the onion mixture. Toss well and cool. Add the scallions, corn, Mozzarella, tomatoes, chives and salt and pepper to taste, and toss well.

Perfect as a cold salad on a hot day.

Duck and Orange Salad

Serves 4.

2 tablespoons fresh orange juice

1 tablespoon soy sauce

2 large duck breast fillets

1 orange (flesh and zest)

pepper

1 tablespoon sunflower oil

4 baby pak choi, trimmed and halved
   lengthwise

4 ounces/110 g fresh beansprouts

4 spring onions, trimmed and finely sliced
   diagonally

FOR THE DRESSING

1 tablespoon fresh orange juice

2 teaspoons peeled and grated fresh root
   ginger

4 tablespoons sunflower oil

dash of soy sauce

squeeze of lemon juice

freshly ground black pepper

Machu Picchu, Peru

Mix the orange juice and soy sauce in a jug. Score the duck skin in a diamond pattern and place the fillets in a shallow dish. Pour over the orange and soy sauce. Refrigerate for 20 minutes.

Meanwhile, make the dressing. Mix the orange juice, grated root ginger, sunflower oil, soy sauce and lemon juice in a bowl. Season with freshly ground black pepper and reserve.

Peel the orange with a serrated knife, removing all the pith. Cut the flesh into segments by running the knife against the membranes to give pith and skin-free pieces. Discard the membranes and reserve the flesh.

Preheat a heavy-based pan and cook the duck fillets, skin side down first, until lightly brown and glazed. Turn over to cook the other side, taking care not to overcook the flesh, and keeping the duck pink in the centre. Season with freshly ground black pepper. Remove from the pan and reserve, keeping warm.

In a separate pan, heat 1 tablespoon sunflower oil. Add the pak choi and toss around to wilt leaves, then remove from heat and reserve.

Place the beansprouts, spring onions and orange zest and segments in a bowl. Slice the cooked and reserved duck breast fillets and add to the bowl. Pour over the dressing and toss to coat and combine.

To serve, divide the pak choi between 4 plates and heap the duck salad on top.

Gina Stewart's
Thai Beef Salad

We were miles from anywhere in the outback of Moree, a cotton growing area in New South Wales, Australia. Tim, a good friend, and I were visiting his sister, Gina. In the heat of the day she cooked this refreshing Thai Beef Salad, which is one of the best I have tasted. She was kind enough to share the recipe with me and it has become frequently used in my kitchen.

2 pounds/910 g lean sirloin, rump or fillet

1/4 cup coriander leaves, chopped

2 cloves garlic, chopped

2 tablespoons soy sauce

2 tablespoons fresh lime or lemon juice

1 tablespoon fish sauce

1 ounce/30 g brown sugar

1/4 cup fresh mint leaves

lettuce leaves

2 shallots, thinly sliced

4 red chillies, cut into strips

1 punnet cherry tomatoes

Fry the steak rare to medium and put aside to cool.

Mix the coriander leaves, garlic, soy sauce, lime juice, fish sauce and sugar in a food processor, blending to a smooth paste. Slice the cooled beef as thinly as possible. Toss in the marinade paste with half the mint leaves.

Arrange the lettuce leaves on a platter. Top with beef, then scatter the shallots, chillies, cherry tomatoes and remaining mint leaves on top before serving. Perfect for a hot summer's day.

Pomelo Salad

1 pomelo

shallot and garlic crisps

shredded coconut meat, dry-fried without oil

1 stalk lemon grass, thick end only, finely sliced

juice of 1 lime

shredded lime leaves

chicken shredded off 1 boiled backbone

1/4 can (14 ounces/400 g) coconut milk

2 teaspoons palm sugar

2 tablespoons tamarind paste, mixed with water and strained for juice

1/2 teaspoon Thai chilli paste (nam prik pao)

1/2 tablespoon fish sauce

1 tablespoon chopped peanuts, for topping

Peel the pomelo and separate the segments. Remove the membranes from the flesh, and break the flesh into smaller pieces, handling carefully so that you do not mash the pulp.

Toss all the other ingredients together, and blend well. Add the pomelo flesh to this mixture and top with chopped peanuts.

Thai Chicken Salad

Serves 1.

1 clove garlic

3–4 green bird chillies

1 teaspoon Thai fish sauce (nam pla)

2 tablespoons lemon juice

$1/2$ teaspoon honey

$3^1/2$ ounces/100 g tomato

$3^1/2$ ounces/100 g chicken meat, cooked

1 stalk celery, finely sliced

2 ounces/50 g onion, finely sliced

1 stalk spring onion, finely sliced

$1/3$ ounce/10 g Chinese parsley, chopped

chives, snipped

coriander, snipped

Crush the garlic and chillies together. Add the fish sauce, lemon juice and honey and mix well together. De-seed the tomato, discarding the seeds, and slice the flesh. Set aside.

Tear the cooked chicken into strips and mix with the celery, onion, spring onion, parsley, chives, coriander and tomato. Add the garlic-chilli dressing, toss well and serve immediately.

Pad Thai

$3^1/2$ ounces/100 g vermicelli noodles

2 tablespoons vegetable oil

1 hard beancurd, chopped

$3^1/2$ ounces/100 g prawns, tails left on

2 eggs, beaten

$1/4$ cup dried shrimp, washed and toasted or dry-fried for 2 minutes

beansprouts

chives, cut into $1^1/2$ inch/4 cm lengths

1 teaspoon preserved radish, minced

$1/2$ cup roasted peanuts, slightly pounded

lots of fresh coriander, coarsely chopped

SAUCE (MIX TOGETHER)

2 tablespoons tamarind paste, mixed with water and strained for juice

2 tablespoons lemon juice

2 tablespoons fish sauce

1 teaspoon sugar

PASTE, POUNDED SLIGHTLY

2 cloves garlic

3 shallots

4 chillies

Soak the noodles in warm water for 5 minutes, or cold water for 10 minutes or until soft. Drain. Heat oil in a wok and fry the beancurd until brown. Remove to a dish. Fry the noodles, adding sauce a little at a time as you fry. Remove and reserve.

Add more oil to the wok and fry the pounded paste until shallots are soft, about 2 minutes. Add the prawns and eggs, cook for 4 minutes, then remove.

Put the noodles back into the wok, add the prawn and egg mixture, dried shrimp, beansprouts, chives, preserved radish and peanuts. Stir-fry for 2 minutes before turning onto a serving dish. Garnish with fresh coriander to serve.

Chiangmai, Thailand

Japanese-Style Coleslaw

2 tablespoons sesame seeds

$1^1/_2$ tablespoons fresh lemon juice

$1^1/_2$ tablespoons light soy sauce

$1^1/_2$ tablespoons sesame oil

$^1/_2$ mini cabbage, sliced finely

6 carrots, finely julienned (2 cups)

$4^1/_2$ ounces/125 g daikon radish, peeled and finely julienned

freshly ground pepper

In a small skillet, toast the sesame seeds, stirring occasionally until lightly browned, about 2 minutes.

In a bowl, whisk the lemon juice with the soy sauce and sesame oil. In another bowl, toss the cabbage, carrots and radish. Add the dressing, season with pepper and toss to coat. Sprinkle with sesame seeds and serve.

Pour the dressing over just before serving, to keep vegetables crisp. Serve with teriyaki chicken or beef.

Vietnamese Green Papaya Salad

1 small green or half-ripe papaya

2 small starfruit, 1 cut into julienne strips, the other sliced crosswise

2 small tomatoes, 1 diced, the other sliced

$^1/_4$ cup fresh lime juice

1 tablespoon Vietnamese or Thai fish sauce

1 clove garlic, minced

1 bird or serrano chilli, minced

1 shallot, minced

$^1/_4$ cup dry-roasted peanuts, finely chopped

1 tablespoon roasted rice flour

$^1/_4$ cup coriander leaves

Peel the papaya, slice lengthwise in half, and remove the seeds. Using a coarse grater, grate into a large bowl. Add the julienned starfruit and diced tomato.

In a small bowl, mix together the lime juice, fish sauce, garlic, chilli, shallot and peanuts. Pour over the salad and toss to blend.

Just before serving, sprinkle on the rice flour and top with coriander leaves. Mound the salad on a plate and arrange the starfruit and tomato slices decoratively around it.

Mount Fuji, Japan

Japanese-Style Coleslaw

Greece

Mrs DeStefano's Marinated Shrimp with Orange

Serves 12.

3 pounds/1⅓ kg large shrimp, uncooked, shelled and deveined

4 oranges, peeled and sectioned

4 medium white onions, thinly sliced

1½ cups cider vinegar

1 cup vegetable oil

⅔ cup fresh lemon juice

½ cup tomato ketchup

¼ cup sugar

2 tablespoons drained capers

2 tablespoons minced parsley

2 teaspoons salt

2 teaspoons mustard seeds

1 teaspoon celery seed

¼ teaspoon pepper

2 cloves garlic, crushed

lettuce (optional)

In boiling water, cook the shrimp for 2 minutes only. Rinse with cold water until thoroughly chilled. Drain.

Combine the shrimp, oranges and onions in a large bowl. Mix the remaining ingredients except the lettuce and pour over the shrimp mixture. Cover and refrigerate for 8 hours or overnight, stirring occasionally. Serve in individual bowls or on a bed of lettuce.

Couscous Salad with Peppers, Olives and Pinenuts

Serves 6–8 as a side dish.

2 cups water

⅓ cup currants or raisins

¾ teaspoon salt

4 tablespoons olive oil, preferably extra virgin

1½ cups couscous

2 large cloves garlic, minced

1 small onion, chopped fine

2 tablespoons red wine vinegar

3 red bell peppers, roasted and chopped (see page 39)

½ packed cup small pimento-stuffed green olives, drained and sliced thin

2 tablespoons drained capers

½ cup pinenuts, toasted slightly

½ cup finely chopped fresh parsley leaves, preferably flat-leafed

salt and pepper for seasoning

In a small saucepan, bring the water to the boil with currants or raisins, salt and 1 tablespoon oil. Stir in the couscous and let stand off heat, covered, for 5 minutes. Fluff the couscous with a fork and transfer to a bowl.

In a small skillet, cook the garlic in 2 tablespoons oil over moderate heat, stirring, until pale golden. Add the onion and cook, stirring, until softened. Stir this onion mixture into the couscous with the vinegar, bell peppers, olives, capers, pinenuts, parsley and remaining 1 tablespoon olive oil. Add salt and pepper to taste.

Africa

Red and Green Pepper Salad

Out watching polo in Kenya, a charming Italian man created a wonderful spread of food. This red and green bell pepper salad was just one of the many foods available but I have never forgotten it. Do not be mean with the vinegar, the salad is meant to have a strong taste of it. Allow time for the salad to cool, as it is best served cold.

2 bell peppers (red and green), sliced

2 onions, sliced

olive oil

$^1/_2$ teaspoon oregano

$^1/_2$ teaspoon minced garlic

salt and pepper

1 teaspoon malt vinegar

1 cup tomato purée

1 can (14 ounces/400 g) tomatoes

Sauté the red and green bell peppers with the onions in olive oil. Sweat until well done. Add the oregano, garlic, salt and pepper, then the vinegar, tomato purée and canned tomatoes. Sometimes I add a teaspoon of tomato ketchup to sweeten it.

Red and Green Pepper Salad

BISCUITS & SWEETS

Yangon, Myanmar

Ecuador

HISTORIC HACIENDAS AND INCA TRAILS

In the summer of 2002, my friends Annabelle Bond and Victoria Chin and I went with Sally Vergette, owner of Ride Andes, on a horseback trek across Ecuador. None of us were prepared for seven hours' riding, for eight days straight.

Our ride took us back in time, down ancient Incan and Spanish colonial routes, past the best-preserved haciendas (grand colonial farming estates) of South America, as we traversed the Andean highlands.

We crossed vast plains and pastoral valleys while following the Avenue of Volcanoes, a valley south of Quito leading to Cuenca, riding between mountain ranges, among them nine of Ecuador's ten highest peaks. Half the population lives here, tilling the rich volcanic soil. Skirting the towering, snowcapped peaks of Cayambe and Cotopaxi, we galloped over the meadows below, through a herd of wild horses who were curious to know what we were doing there.

Our days were packed with fascinating rides through forests and up into the mountains, along Inca roads, with stops at the local markets and craft villages where the customs and rhythm of life have changed little over the centuries.

After six hours' hard trekking, two of which consisted of solid cantering along extremely dusty roads and over metal bridges, with laundry flapping into our horses' faces, scaring them, we felt lucky just to get to our beds alive each night. The horses were of excellent quality – fast, frisky and hard to stop. Our utmost attention was required to keep their feet steady on the narrow, steep and slippery paths.

At the end of each hard day we were thrilled to see our haciendas, dating from the 16th to 18th century. Each was unique, allowing us to relax before open fireplaces, luxuriating in the fine period detail. The haciendas we stayed at hold an important place in the history of Ecuador. Many are still the homes of noble Ecuadorian families, including past presidents and famous guests like Simon Bolívar.

Ecuador holds a magical beauty. The people are welcoming and so patriotic. Seeing the country on horseback was fun and exhilarating… I shall certainly return.

Vermont Cranberry and Oat Bran Scones

These to-die-for scones were discovered in the famous Old Drove Inn in Vermont. Serve warm with double cream and strawberry jam.

Makes 12 to 24 scones depending on shape and size.

1^1/$_2$ cups dried cranberries

3 cups all-purpose flour

1 cup Old Fashioned Rolled Oats, ground in processor to a fine texture

^{1}/$_4$ cup light brown sugar

2 tablespoons baking powder

^{1}/$_2$ teaspoon iodised table salt

^{1}/$_2$ cup plus 1 tablespoon unsalted butter, cold and cut into cubes

1^1/$_2$ cups buttermilk

Preheat the oven to 400°F/200°C/Gas 6. Place the cranberries in a small bowl and cover with boiling water.

Combine the flour, processed oats, brown sugar, baking powder and salt. Cut in the pieces of butter with a pastry knife or with fingertips until the flour has the texture of coarse crumbs. Make a well in the centre of the flour mixture. Drain the cranberries (discard the water) and add to the mixture with the buttermilk. Stir until a sticky dough is formed.

Turn the dough out onto a floured surface, preferably a wooden board, then knead gently until it holds together. Do not overwork the dough or it loses its tender, flaky crumb. Pat into a 1 inch/2^1/$_2$ cm thick circle, then cut into traditional triangles, or pat into a 1 inch/2^1/$_2$ cm rectangle and cut with a cutter of desired size and shape.

Place the scones on a sheetpan covered with parchment paper, or on a non-stick pan. Brush them with heavy cream, then sprinkle with rolled oats, brown sugar, raw sugar or castor sugar. Bake until golden brown, about 10–15 minutes. Serve with butter, jam or preserves.

Toffee Krispies

9 ounces/250 g bag toffees

2 ounces/50 g butter

3 tablespoons milk

4 ounces/110 g marshmallows

6 ounces/170 g rice krispies

Oil a tin. Put the toffee, butter and milk in a saucepan. Heat until melted. Add the marshmallows and rice krispies and mix until melted. Put into a tin to cool. Cut into squares and serve in a small paper cake mould at a children's tea party.

Honeycomb

I have always had a sweet tooth and this honeycomb is guaranteed to pull it out! It is hard to locate liquid glucose these days but sometimes Boots the chemist store does sell it. I sometimes serve this with coffee at the end of a dinner party.

11^1/$_2$ ounces/325 g castor sugar

2 ounces/50 g light honey

4^1/$_2$ ounces/125 g liquid glucose

2 fl. ounces/60 ml water

^{1}/$_2$ ounce/15 g bicarbonate of soda

Line a workbench with baking paper. Bring the castor sugar, honey, liquid glucose and water to the boil in a large saucepan. Cook over moderately high heat until the mixture becomes golden brown, like caramel. Add the bicarbonate of soda and whisk quickly. The mixture will look like molten lava at this stage – it more than doubles in volume, so make sure you are working in a suitable-sized pan. Pour the mixture onto the lined workbench, then allow it to cool and set. This will take only about 15 minutes.

Remove the paper, break the honeycomb into manageable pieces and store in an airtight container well away from heat until ready to use. To serve as a petit four, break the honeycomb into shards.

Anne Bosomworth's Highlander Biscuits and Oat Biscuits

Anne Bosomworth's Highlander Biscuits

Anne Bosomworth is one of my best-loved people in the world. She has been generous in revealing many of her kitchen secrets, all of which I love. Here are just a couple of her homemade biscuits. The oat biscuits are a particular favourite and whenever we get to see each other around the world, Anne always arrives with a box in hand!

10 ounces/280 g plain flour

4 ounces/110 g icing sugar

4 ounces/110 g butter

4 ounces/110 g margarine

demerara sugar

Sieve the flour and icing sugar and add butter and margarine. Knead well. Roll into 2 long rolls. Refrigerate till firm. Roll in demerara sugar and cut into rounds 1/2 inch/1 cm thick. Bake at 325°F/170°F/ Gas 3 for 20–30 minutes or until brown.

Anne Bosomworth's Oat Biscuits

2 ounces/50 g plain flour

2 ounces/50 g self-raising flour

8 ounces/225 g castor sugar

8 ounces/225 g margarine

12 ounces/340 g oats (quick-cooking)

Sieve the flour and castor sugar and add the margarine, then the oats. Knead well, making sure that the margarine is evenly distributed. Pour the mixture onto a well-buttered/floured flat baking tray.

Press the biscuit mixture firmly and evenly around the tin so there are no air pockets. Flatten evenly with a fork so the surface is smooth. Bake at 325°F/170°C/ Gas 3 for 15–25 minutes or until golden brown.

Cut the biscuits into rectangles and allow to cool on an iron rack.

Serves perfectly with a nice cup of tea!

Chocolate Pecan Biscuits

Makes 2 to 3 dozen pieces.

8 ounces/225 g unsalted butter, at room temperature, plus more for the pan

1/3 cup water

1 cup sugar

2 cups chopped pecans, plus more halves (optional) for top

8 ounces/225 g semisweet chocolate (optional)

2 tablespoons light corn syrup (optional)

Butter a 9 inch/23 cm square baking pan, and line the bottom with a piece of parchment paper that extends up and over two sides. Butter the parchment, and set the pan aside.

Place the butter and water in a large saucepan. Cook at high heat until the butter is melted. Add the sugar, and stir constantly until dissolved and the mixture comes to the boil. Using a pastry brush dipped in water, brush away any sugar crystals on the side of the pan to prevent recrystallisation. Cook until the mixture is dark amber in colour. Remove from heat and stir in pecans. Pour into the prepared baking pan, and let stand at room temperature to cool completely.

Place the chocolate and corn syrup, if using, in a small heatproof bowl set over a pan of barely simmering water. Stir occasionally until combined and completely melted. Let cool slightly, and spread over the top of the cooled toffee. Arrange the pecan halves on top, and let sit at room temperature until the chocolate has cooled completely and set, at least 2 hours or overnight. Unmould carefully by lifting out the parchment paper. Break or cut into pieces, and store in an airtight container at room temperature for up to 1 month.

Scotland

Brandysnap Baskets

I have always loved brandysnaps but they are sometimes complicated to make. I have found this easy-to-use recipe which has never failed me. Remember to roll the mixture around a cup quickly before the substance hardens.

Serves 4.

4 ounces/110 g fresh brown breadcrumbs

2 ounces/50 g soft brown sugar

1/2 pint/240 ml double cream

1/4 pint/120 ml single cream

1 tablespoon rum

1 ounce/30 g icing sugar

FOR THE BASKETS

1 ounce/30 g butter

1 ounce/30 g castor sugar

1 tablespoon golden syrup

1 ounce/30 g flour

1/4 teaspoon ground ginger

2–3 pieces stem ginger, cut into shreds, to decorate

mint leaves, to decorate

Make the ice cream the day before the meal. Preheat the oven to 400°F/200°C/Gas 6. Mix together the breadcrumbs and soft brown sugar and spread over a baking tray. Bake in the oven for about 10 minutes. Cool, then crumble between your fingers.

Whisk together the double and single cream until just stiff. Fold in the rum and icing sugar, and spoon into a container. Freeze for 2 hours.

Place the cream mixture in a mixing bowl and beat well until smooth. Stir in the breadcrumbs and return to container. Freeze until firm.

Preheat the oven to 350°F/180°C/Gas 4. Line a baking tray with baking parchment. Melt the butter, sugar and syrup over low heat. Beat in the flour and ginger, then leave to cool.

Divide the mixture into 4, roll into balls and place on a baking tray about 4 inches/10 cm apart. Flatten each ball into 4 inches/10 cm rounds and bake for 7–10 minutes or until golden and bubbly. Set out 4 teacups upside down.

Allow the biscuits to cool slightly. Then, quickly and carefully, remove each one with a palette knife and lay over the upturned teacups. Mould the biscuits into basket shapes and then leave them to cool and harden.

To serve, scoop 2–3 balls of ice cream into each basket and decorate with the stem ginger and mint leaves.

Daisy Paciente's Philippine Toffees

Daisy often makes these sweets for me. I love them, but they are dangerous for the teeth!

1 can (14 ounces/400g) condensed milk

1 egg yolk

1 tablespoon vegetable oil

3 cups granulated sugar

toothpicks

Pour the condensed milk with the egg yolk into a bowl and mix well. Transfer this mixture to a nonstick heavy frying pan already brushed with 1 tablespoon oil. Cook the mixture slowly on very low heat so that it does not burn. Stir continuously until it looks like thick, soft dough. Transfer the mixture onto a greased plate and allow it to cool slightly so you can handle it. Make small 1/2 inch/1 cm balls and line them on a shallow baking pan (greased and lined with tin foil). Insert a toothpick into each ball.

Put 3 cups of sugar into a small, heavy saucepan. Cook on medium heat, stirring continuously until the sugar dissolves and turns light brown, but do not burn the syrup. Using the toothpicks, dip each toffee ball into the syrup, making sure that they are well covered with the syrup. Place them to cool on a baking tray covered with foil. (Make sure they are spaced out so they don't stick to each other.) Store in an airtight box or wrap individually with plastic wrappers.

PUDDINGS & CAKES

Polynesia, Fiji

Mary Mitchell's Clooty Dumpling from Dalvanie

Mary, sister of Anne Bosomworth (see Highlander Biscuits) kindly passed on this historical recipe which has been passed down through the generations of her own family. A traditional Scottish recipe, this is an all-time favourite of my father's: he often gets to scrounge a bite of this delicious pudding when in Scotland for the Glenisla Games.

1 pound/450 g plain flour

8 ounces/225 g suet (vegetarian) or margarine

4 ounces/110 g sugar

1 pound/450 g raisins

8 ounces/225 g sultanas

1 level teaspoon baking soda

2 level teaspoons cream of tartar

1 level teaspoon ginger

1 level teaspoon mixed spice

1 level teaspoon cinnamon

2 large tablespoons treacle

1 egg

milk

Mix all the ingredients with enough milk to make a stiff dough.

Turn the mixture onto a prepared wet muslin square, generously dusted with flour. The muslin forms a seal and skin around the dumpling. Tie up firmly with string, leaving just enough room for the dumpling to rise (folds in the cloth give almost sufficient extra space).

Boil for 4 hours in a large pan of already boiling water.

When cooked, turn out the dumpling onto a plate (like a Christmas pudding) and serve with lashings of cream.

Creamy Passionfruit Mousse

Serves 4–6.

$^1/_2$ cup castor sugar

$^1/_2$ cup strained passionfruit juice

4 egg yolks

6 teaspoons powdered gelatine dissolved in $^1/_3$ cup sherry

10 fl. ounces/300 ml thick cream

4 egg whites, beaten with a pinch of salt until soft peaks form

whipped cream

pulp of 6 passionfruit, sweetened with some castor sugar to taste

In a bowl, beat together the sugar, passionfruit juice, egg yolks, gelatine and sherry, until well combined. Place over a saucepan of simmering water and beat until the mixture reaches the consistency of custard, then set it aside until it gets completely cold, stirring occasionally.

Stir the thick cream into the cold custard and carefully fold through the beaten egg whites. Pour the mousse into a serving bowl and chill in the refrigerator until firm.

Serve the mousse with whipped cream and passionfruit pulp spooned over the top.

Liz Seaton's Mango and Passionfruit Pavlova

Liz Seaton's Mango and Passionfruit Pavlova

Another of Liz Seaton's classics. This is one of my favourite puddings, that can be served either as one large pavlova, or small individual ones, as I do when I throw a formal dinner party.

Makes 12 pieces.

FOR THE MERINGUE

non-stick baking paper

4 egg whites

pinch of salt

8 ounces/225 g castor sugar

$1^1/_4$ level teaspoons cornflour

$1^1/_4$ teaspoons vinegar

PASTRY CREAM

3 egg yolks

4 ounces/110 g castor sugar

2 ounces/50 g white or wholemeal flour

2 cups whole or skimmed milk

vanilla pod or essence

TOPPINGS

1 large round cooked meringue

4 mangoes, sliced

4 passionfruit (mix with pastry cream)

First of all, preheat the oven to 250°F/130°C/Gas $^1/_2$.

MERINGUE

Line the baking sheet with non-stick baking paper and set aside. Put the egg whites and salt in a large bowl, and whisk until stiff. Add half the sugar and continue whisking until glossy. With a large metal spoon, fold in the remaining sugar, cornflour and vinegar. Spoon the meringue onto the baking sheet. Hollow out the centre of the mounds with the back of a spoon to make a nest shape.

Bake the meringue in the oven for 1 hour until crisp outside. Lift the meringue case from the baking paper with a fish knife and place on a wire rack to cool.

PASTRY CREAM

Whisk the eggs and sugar in a bowl until almost white. Mix in the flour. Boil the milk in a thick-based pan. Whisk onto the eggs, sugar and flour and mix well. Return to the cleaned pan, stir to the boil. Add a few drops of vanilla essence or vanilla pod. Mix until thick, then cool. Add the passionfruit pulp onto the pastry cream mixture.

Lay the meringue in a large cake platter. Layer with the whipped cream, sliced mango, then pastry cream, and another layer of sliced mango on top. Sprinkle with icing sugar.

Lemon Mousse

Serves 8.

3 egg yolks

3 tablespoons honey

2 teaspoons powdered gelatine

$^1/_3$ cup water

$^1/_3$ cup lemon juice

$6^3/_4$ fl. ounces/200 ml evaporated milk, chilled

3 egg whites

$^1/_2$ cup sugar

Beat the yolks and honey until pale. Sprinkle the gelatine over water and let it swell for 5 minutes, then microwave on Medium for 10 seconds. Stir and leave a further 10 seconds to fully dissolve. Add lemon juice and stir into beaten egg yolk mix. Set aside to thicken.

Beat the milk to soft peaks. Whip the egg whites until soft then slowly add sugar to make a soft white meringue. Fold cream and meringue into lemon mixture. Spoon into 8 small serving bowls and chill 2–3 hours. Serve garnished with strips of lemon zest.

Coconut Milk Sticky Rice with Mangoes

Serves 8.

3 cups sticky rice, soaked overnight in water or thin coconut milk and drained

2 cups canned or fresh coconut milk

3/4 cup palm sugar (or brown sugar)

1 teaspoon salt

4 ripe mangoes (or ripe peaches or papaya)

mint or basil sprigs for garnish (optional)

Steam the sticky rice until tender, about 30 minutes.

Meanwhile, place the coconut milk in a heavy pot and heat on medium temperature until hot. Do not boil. Add the sugar and salt and stir to dissolve completely.

When the sticky rice is tender, turn it out into a bowl and pour 1 cup of the hot coconut milk over; reserve the rest. Stir to mix the liquid into the rice, then let stand for 20 minutes to an hour to allow the flavours to blend.

Peel the mangoes. The mango pit is flat and you want to slice the mango flesh off the pit as cleanly as possible. One at a time, lay the mangoes on a narrow side of the cutting board and slice lengthwise about 1/2 inch/1 cm from the centre. Your knife should cut just along the flat side of the pit. If it strikes the pit, shift over a fraction more until you can slice downward. Repeat on the other side of the pit, giving you two hemispherical pieces of mango. (The cook gets to snack on the stray bits of mango still clinging to the pit.) Lay each mango half flat and slice thinly crosswise.

To serve individually, place an oval mound of sticky rice on each dessert plate and place a sliced half-mango decoratively beside it. Top with a sprig of mint or basil if you wish. Or place the mango slices on a platter and pass it around, together with a serving bowl containing the rice, allowing guests to serve themselves. Stir the remaining sweetened coconut milk thoroughly, transfer to a small serving bowl or cruet, and pass it separately, with a spoon, so guests can spoon on extra as they wish.

Warm, Soft Chocolate Cake

This is one of my favourite recipes, which you can find in many restaurants, but this was kindly given by a very special friend, Lucy Bond. This is very easy to make and the result is mouthwatering.

Makes 4 cakes.

1/2 cup/1 stick butter, plus some for buttering the moulds

4 squares (4 ounces/110 g) bittersweet chocolate, preferably Valrhona

2 eggs

2 egg yolks

1/4 cup sugar

2 teaspoons flour, plus more for dusting

Heat the butter and chocolate over simmering water until the chocolate is almost all melted. Beat together the eggs, yolks and sugar until light and thick. Beat together the melted chocolate and butter, pour in the egg mixture, and quickly beat in the flour, until combined.

Butter and lightly flour four 4 ounce/110 g moulds, custard cups or ramekins. Tap out the excess flour, then butter and flour again. Divide the batter among the moulds. (You can chill the desserts for a few hours, but bring back to room temperature before baking.)

Preheat the oven to 450°F/230°C/Gas 8. Bake the batter for 6–7 minutes; the centre will still be quite soft, but the sides will be set.

Invert each mould onto a plate and let sit for about 10 seconds. Unmould by lifting up a corner; the cake will fall out onto the plate. Serve immediately.

Lime and Ginger Rice Pudding

Lime and Ginger Rice Pudding

Serves 4–6.

1 cup milk

^{1}/$_2$ cup cream

^{1}/$_2$ cup sugar

6 pieces crystallised ginger, sliced

zest of 2 limes

3 cups cooked short-grain rice, well drained

2 eggs, beaten

vanilla ice cream, to serve

Preheat the oven to 325°F/170°F/Gas 3. Place the milk, cream, sugar and ginger in a saucepan and heat to near boiling. Remove from heat and add the lime zest. Cool slightly, then mix in the rice and beaten eggs. Pour into a shallow ovenproof 9 inch/23 cm glass dish and bake for 20–25 minutes until set and just starting to caramelise. Serve warm with ice cream.

Aunty Joy's Christmas Pudding

As a child I was privy to many of my aunt's secrets of good home cooking. This recipe is one of my mother's favourites. It is unique in that you can cook it the day before, and there is no suet in the ingredients.

Serves 6–8.

6 ounces/170 g large seedless raisins

4 ounces/110 g currants

4 ounces/110 g sultanas

4 ounces/110 g grated carrot

4 ounces/110 g fresh breadcrumbs

2 ounces/50 g plain flour

4 ounces/110 g chilled or frozen butter, grated

4 ounces/110 g soft light brown sugar

1 ounce/30 g toasted flaked almonds

1 teaspoon ground mixed spices

rind of 1 lemon

3 tablespoons thick-cut marmalade

2 eggs, beaten

2 fl. ounces/60 ml brandy or whiskey

Put all the ingredients in a large bowl and mix thoroughly until evenly combined. Butter a 2 pint/1 litre pudding basin and spoon in the mixture. Level the top.

Fold a pleat each in a piece of grease-proof paper and a piece of foil. Lay one on top of the other. Place the paper side down on the pudding basin and tie some string around the rim of the basin to secure it. Place in a large saucepan or pressure cooker.

There are several ways to cook this.

To steam, pour boiling water into the pan until it comes halfway up the pudding basin. Bring to the boil, then reduce heat and simmer gently (4–5 hours if making ahead of time, 5–6 hours if cooking on Christmas morning). Steam for 1 hour to reheat.

If pressure cooking, pre-steam for 20 minutes, then cook for 2–3 hours on high pressure. Cook on high pressure to reheat.

In a microwave, you will not get the caramelised effect, but if you cook it in advance you can reheat by microwaving on medium-high for 4–5 minutes. Remove the greaseproof paper and foil and cover with cling film first.

This pudding will keep for up to 6 months in a cool, dark, well ventilated place, and up to 1 year if you freeze it.

Scotland

Chocolate Mousse

8 ounces/225 g milk chocolate

butter

4 eggs, separated

drop of brandy

Melt the chocolate with a little butter over a bowl of hot water. Add the egg yolks and cream them together gently. Add a drop of brandy. Whisk the egg whites until firm and fold gently into the chocolate mousse. Leave to cool in the fridge before serving.

Lemon and Blueberry Bread and Butter Pudding

Serves 6–8.

16–20 slices stale white bread, crusts removed

3–4 ounces/85–110 g cultured unsalted butter, at room temperature

2 punnets blueberries (or use 12$^1/_2$– 14 ounces/350–400 g frozen berries)

1 tablespoon finely chopped lemon zest

CUSTARD

3 eggs

3 egg yolks, extra

1 cup castor sugar

2$^1/_2$ cups milk

$^1/_2$ cup cream

3$^1/_3$ fl. ounces/100 ml lemon juice, strained

TO SERVE

icing sugar, for dusting

cream

If the bread slices are large, halve or quarter them. Lightly butter one side of each slice.

Butter a medium-sized, deep ovenproof dish. Put a layer of bread slices, buttered side down in the bottom. Sprinkle some of the blueberries and zest over the bread. Repeat this layering 4 or 5 times, depending on the shape of the dish. For a pretty top layer, use a large scone cutter to cut rounds from the buttered bread and overlap these on top. If you do this, you may need a bit more bread and butter. Finish off with the last of the blueberries and lemon.

To make the custard, lightly whisk together the eggs, extra yolks and sugar until well combined. Whisk in the milk and cream, then slowly drizzle in the lemon juice, whisking all the while.

Pour this mixture through a fine sieve evenly over the pudding. Cover the pudding loosely with plastic wrap and press down gently on the surface to partially submerge the bread. Leave it to stand and cool at room temperature for at least 2 hours, or in the fridge overnight, but return it to room temperature before cooking.

Preheat the oven to 350°F/180°C/ Gas 4. Remove the plastic wrap and sit the pudding dish in a large baking tin. Put the tin on the middle rack of the oven and carefully pour enough boiling water into it to reach halfway up the sides of the pudding dish. Bake the pudding for 50–60 minutes, or until the top is slightly puffed and golden with some dark, crispy bits. Check the pudding after 35 minutes. If the top is quite golden brown, loosely cover it with foil. The cooking time will vary according to the size and shape of your dish.

Dust with icing sugar, and serve with cream.

Tirol, Austria

Alex Appelby's Strawberry Ice Cream

A deliciously simple ice cream to make which was kindly given to me by Alex, a dear friend from Hong Kong. Serve with fresh strawberries.

Makes approximately 1¼ pints/600 ml.

1 pound/450 g ripe strawberries

4 ounces/110 g castor sugar

1 cup double cream

juice of 1 lemon

Mash the strawberries or purée them in a processor. Mix the sugar, cream and lemon juice. Taste for sweetness before freezing in an ice cream machine.

Mummy's Danish Fruit Salad

This recipe originated from Denmark and has now been in my family for many years. We used to eat this every Sunday after a roast dinner. It is important to remember to include the ice cream and chunks of chocolate. Delicious but very rich. Sprinkle grated chocolate on the top for decoration.

½ can (10 ounces/280 g) fruit cocktail (or tin of peaches or real fresh fruit, depending on time of year)

handful of fresh grapes

1 bar of wholenut chocolate

4 egg whites

½ pint/240 ml double cream

2 ounces/50 g castor sugar

block of vanilla ice cream

Strain the fruits or cut into small pieces, and take out the pips from the grapes. Break up the chocolate, and whisk the egg whites until firm. Whip the double cream. Stir the sugar and cream into the egg whites, and add the fruit, chocolate and grapes. Cut up the ice cream into cubes, then stir into the fruit salad. Sprinkle chocolate over the top before serving.

Mummy's Danish Fruit Salad

Hot Toffee Soufflé

Hot Toffee Soufflé

Serves 6.

FOR THE PRALINE

oil for greasing

1 ounce/30 g blanched, peeled almonds

1 ounce/30 g castor sugar, plus extra for
    dusting

butter for greasing

FOR THE TOFFEE SAUCE

$^1/_2$ ounce/15 g butter

$^3/_4$ ounce/20 g soft brown sugar

2 tablespoons golden syrup

1 cup milk

3 large eggs, separated

2 ounces/50 g castor sugar

1 ounce/30 g flour

Oil a baking tray and make the praline. Put the almonds and castor sugar into a small heavy-based pan and place over low heat. Leave until the sugar is melted and golden brown, then pour onto the baking tray. Allow to harden, then grind coarsely in a food processor.

Now, preheat the oven to 425°F/220°C/ Gas 7. Position a baking tray on the centre shelf. Brush six $3^1/_2$ inch/9 cm ramekins with butter and then dust the inside of each one with castor sugar.

To make the toffee sauce, put the butter, soft brown sugar and golden syrup in a small saucepan and set over low heat until melted. Boil for 2 minutes, then cool slightly.

Meanwhile, quickly bring the milk to the boil and set aside. Beat the egg yolks and half the castor sugar until pale. Beat in the flour and then the hot milk. Pour the mixture back into the saucepan and simmer for 2 minutes, stirring constantly. Remove from heat to cool slightly, then mix in the toffee sauce.

Whisk the egg whites until stiff and then whisk in the remaining castor sugar. Fold a large spoonful of the egg white mixture into the coffee mixture, then lightly fold in the remainder.

Spoon the mixture into the prepared ramekins and sprinkle the top of each with 1 teaspoonful of the praline. Place on the preheated baking tray and bake for 10–12 minutes.

Poached Pears with Raspberry Sauce

Serves 6.

15 fl. ounces/440 ml water

15 fl. ounces/440 ml dry white wine

10 ounces/280 g castor sugar

juice of 1 lemon

6 firm pears, peeled with stalks on

FOR THE SAUCE

7 ounces/200 g fresh raspberries

2 ounces/50 g castor sugar

Mix water, wine, sugar and juice of one lemon in a saucepan. Peel the pears, then add to the mixture. Do this quickly to prevent the pears from discolouring. Place it over medium heat and cook until the pears are just soft. Remove the pear from the cooking liquid and drain.

To make the sauce, mix the raspberries with sugar in a saucepan. Simmer for 3 minutes or until the sugar dissolves. Pass through a fine sieve into a clean bowl.

Place one pear on each plate, then pour the sauce around the pears and garnish with mint leaves.

Poached Pears with Raspberry Sauce

Lemon Delicious

Serves 6.

2 ounces/50 g butter, softened

3/4 cup castor sugar

finely grated zest of 1 lemon

3 eggs, separated

3 tablespoons self-raising flour

1 1/4 cups milk

juice of 2 lemons

Preheat the oven to 325°F/170°C/Gas 3 and butter 6 small ramekins. Cream the butter and sugar. Beat in the zest and egg yolks. Gently fold in the flour, milk and lemon juice.

In a separate bowl, beat the egg whites until lightly stiff. Gently fold the lemon mixture into the egg whites a third at a time. Spoon into ramekins and stand them in an oven dish. Place in the oven and pour in hot water to come halfway up the sides of the ramekins. Bake about 35 minutes or until the puddings are golden and risen. Serve immediately, dusted with icing sugar.

Fig and Macadamia Pudding

This recipe was discovered in Margaret River, Perth. I love figs, and macadamia more, so this was a perfect recipe. Very filling and quite sweet, so I tend to make just small little puddings rather than one large one.

1 1/2 pounds/680 g dried figs

2 teaspoons bicarbonate of soda

4 cups water

1 1/2 pounds/680 g brown sugar

8 1/2 ounces/240 g unsalted butter

2 teaspoons vanilla essence

8 eggs, beaten

1 1/2 pounds/680 g self-raising flour

13 ounces/370 g macadamia nuts

SAUCE

10 ounces/280 g unsalted butter

10 ounces/280 g brown sugar

15 fl. ounces/440 ml cream

Put the figs and soda bicarbonate in water in a large pot and bring to the boil. Simmer for 5 minutes. Add the brown sugar, butter and vanilla essence to the fig mixture. Add the beaten eggs and fold in the flour and macadamia nuts.

Put the mixture into lined and well-greased cake tins or small pudding moulds. Bake at 275°F/140°C/Gas 1 for 1 hour if using cake tins, and for 30–40 minutes if using small moulds.

Meanwhile, prepare the sauce. Melt the butter and add the sugar. Cook slowly over low heat for 2–3 minutes until the sugar has melted. Cool before adding the cream.

Serve the pudding on individual dessert plates with the sauce.

Mummy's Cheesecake

Another classic recipe from Mummy. An easy, no-fuss cheesecake that always turns out just right. This freezes beautifully, but improves in flavour if left a day or two in the fridge.

half packet digestive biscuits or Graham crackers

4 ounces/110 g butter

3 ounces/85 g sugar

2-3 eggs

2 packets Philadelphia cream cheese

vanilla essence

lemon, juice and grated peel

1 tub (12 ounces/340 g) sour cream

Crush the biscuits over melted butter and mould into a 1 inch/2$^1/_2$ cm deep pie dish. Bake in an oven at 350°F/180°C/Gas 4 for 10 minutes.

While the pie base is baking, put two-thirds of the sugar into a bowl, add the eggs, and whisk until white and frothy. Add the cream cheese, 4 drops of vanilla essence, a little lemon juice and the grated lemon peel. Mix to a fine consistency. Pour into the pie mould and put back into the oven for about 20 minutes. Do not overcook, as this pie is better underdone than over. You can test it by pressing a finger on the mixture. It should just make an impression. Take out and cool.

For the topping, whisk the sour cream with remaining sugar, lemon juice and vanilla essence. Pour over the cake, smooth it and use a fork to pattern. Scatter candied fruit or leave plain.

Key Lime Pie

I found this recipe on Palm Island in Florida. It is hard to get the Graham crackers but when you make your first pie I promise this will become a favourite. Once, sailing in Hong Kong, I took this pie as part of a picnic I had prepared; we literally had boats from all angles sailing up just to try a piece!

Makes 2 pies.

FOR THE CRUST

4 cups cashew or macadamia nuts, chopped

2 cups Graham cracker crumbs

1 cup sugar

1$^1/_2$ cups melted butter

FOR THE KEY LIME MIXTURE

6$^1/_4$ cups sweetened condensed milk

18 egg yolks

3$^3/_4$ cups key lime juice

FOR THE TOPPING

2 gelatin sheets

4 cups heavy cream

4 ounces/110 g sugar

zest of 2 oranges

Belize

First, make the crust by mixing all the crust ingredients in a pie dish, together with the melted butter, and parbaking in a 325°F/170°C/Gas 3 oven till golden.

Make the key lime mixture. Combine the condensed milk and egg yolks, adding the eggs slowly. Then add the key lime juice slowly. Pour the mixture over the parbaked crust and bake in a 300°F/150°C/Gas 2 oven about 20 minutes or until the centre is set.

Prepare the topping. First soften gelatin sheets in water per instructions on the packet. Add to the cream and whip with sugar until firm. Fold in the chopped orange zest and cover the top of the pie.

Chilled Strawberry Soufflé

Serves 8.

8 ounces/225 g strawberries

2 ounces/50 g unrefined castor sugar

5 fl. ounces/150 ml water

3 leaves of gelatine

10 fl. ounces/300 ml double cream, Jersey if you can get it

whites of 4 organic eggs

Liquidise the raw strawberries, or push them through a nylon sieve. Make a syrup by heating the sugar and water then, when it has cooled slightly, dissolve the gelatine in it. Sieve the syrup and the dissolved gelatine into the strawberry liquid, stirring well, then fold in the lightly whipped cream and put it in the fridge until chilled and just beginning to set.

Whisk the egg whites until they stand in stiff peaks. Cut a tablespoon of the whites into the mixture using a spoon, then fold in the rest of the whites gradually and lightly.

Cut a double strip of greaseproof paper long enough to wrap around a 1 pint/470 ml soufflé dish with the ends slightly overlapping, and high enough to stand up like a collar, 2$\frac{1}{3}$ inches/6 cm above the rim. Turn the mixture into the dish and pile it to the top of the greaseproof paper collar, or heap it into individual glasses and refrigerate until set. Remove the paper collar from the soufflé dish before serving.

Lyn Pooley's Lemon Sponge Pudding

I love this recipe during winter after an English roast. It is very filling, so serve only small portions, with lashings of cream.

2 ounces/50 g butter

juice and grated rind of 1 lemon

3 ounces/80 g castor sugar

2 eggs, separated

1 ounce/30 g plain flour

$\frac{3}{4}$ cup milk

Cream the butter with the lemon rind and sugar until light and fluffy. Mix in the egg yolks, flour and lemon juice, then stir in the milk. Whisk the egg whites till stiff, and fold the egg white into the batter.

Turn onto a greased ovenproof dish. Place the dish in a roasting tin and add 1 inch/2$\frac{1}{2}$ cm of water to the tin. Bake for 40–45 minutes in a 350°F/180°C/Gas 4 oven.

Serve hot with lashings of single cream.

Lyn Pooley's Lemon Sponge Pudding

Afghanistan

Mrs Wigmore's Chocolate Gateau

4 ounces/110 g soft margarine

4 tablespoons golden syrup

4 tablespoons drinking chocolate powder

4 ounces/110 g self-raising flour

1 level teaspoon baking powder

2 tablespoons cocoa

4 eggs

1 dessertspoon warm water

BUTTER ICING

4 ounces/110 g margarine

8 ounces/225 g icing sugar

1 tablespoon cocoa or chocolate powder

Warm a bowl, and cream the margarine till soft. Add the syrup and drinking chocolate powder and beat well. Sieve the flour, baking powder and cocoa and add to the creamed mixture alternately with the eggs. Stir in warm water.

Divide the batter into two greased and lined 8 inch/20 cm tins and bake at 350°F/180°F/Gas 4 for 25 minutes. Turn onto a rack to cool.

Prepare the icing. Mix the margarine with the icing sugar and cocoa. Sandwich the icing between the two cakes, then spread it on the sides and top. Sprinkle chocolate on the top.

Granny Lee's Temby Cream Lemon Pudding

1 pint milk (sometimes I use $^3/_4$ cup of single cream, $^1/_2$ cup of milk)

2–3 lemons, for juice and rind

6 ounces/170 g castor sugar

$^1/_2$ ounce gelatine

2 eggs, separated and the whites whisked till stiff

Put the milk, lemon rind, sugar and gelatine in a saucepan and place on the lowest heat possible until it dissolves. It is important not to boil this mixture. Strain the mixture so that the lemon rind is removed. Add the beaten egg yolks and return to the heat, barely bringing to the boil and just enough so that the milk cracks. Add the strained lemon juice and fold in the whisked egg whites. Place into either one large glass bowl or individual glass ramekin bowls so that you are able to see the separation of the mixture and egg whites. Refrigerate for 2–4 hours and serve cold with cream.

Summer Pudding

This is a very old traditional English recipe that is seldom used these days, but whenever I prepare it all my friends seem to enjoy it. It is best to use stale bread. Serve with plenty of cream.

10 thick slices white bread

10 ounces/280 g punnet strawberries

10 ounces/280 g punnet raspberries

10 ounces/280 g punnet redcurrants

$3/4$ cup castor sugar

1 tablespoon Framboise (raspberry-flavoured liqueur)

Line pudding mould with foil.

Trim the crusts from the bread. Reserve 2 slices, and cut the remaining slices into 3 fingers. Line the base of the mould with 1 reserved slice, and cut to fit the base. Line the sides of the mould with some of the bread fingers, overlapping slightly.

Combine the berries, currants and sugar in a medium saucepan, and stir over heat without boiling until the sugar is dissolved. Bring to the boil, reduce heat and cover. Simmer for about 3 minutes, or until the fruit softens. Stir in the liqueur, strain, and reserve the liquid and fruit.

Brush the bread in the mould with some of the reserved liquid. Spoon the fruit into the mould, top with the reserved bread slice and fingers. Pour the remaining liquid over the bread and cover with

Summer Pudding

foil. Cover with a plate slightly smaller than the mould, place a heavy weight on top, and refrigerate overnight.

Turn the pudding onto a plate and serve with whipped cream if desired.

Sara Hine's Truffle Torte

An old friend from England, Sara, once cooked this at one of her dinner parties. I was so impressed I immediately asked for her recipe. I cook two at a time and leave one in the freezer for when I need it!

3 ounces/85 g amaretti biscuits, crushed finely

1 pound/450 g plain chocolate, broken up

5 tablespoons liquid glucose, warmed till very gooey

5 tablespoons rum

2 cups double cream at room temperature

TO SERVE

cocoa powder for dusting

chilled single cream

Prepare two 8 inch/20 cm tins (each for six people). Line the tins with grease-proof paper and brush the base and sides with oil. Sprinkle amaretti biscuit crumbs over the base of the tin.

Put the chocolate, liquid glucose and rum in a heatproof bowl and sit the bowl over boiling water until chocolate melts. Leave the mixture for 5 minutes to cool.

In a separate bowl, beat the double cream till slightly thickened. Fold half the cream into the chocolate mixture, then fold this mixture into the rest of the cream. Pour into the two tins. Tap the tins to get an even distribution of mixture. Cover with cling film and refrigerate overnight.

Before serving, run a palette knife round the tin and shake the tin. Turn out onto a plate and dust with cocoa powder. Serve with chilled cream.

Ginger Cheesecake

Makes four 4-inch/10-cm cheesecakes.

FOR THE FILLING

$^1/_2$ cup water

$^1/_2$ cup sugar

$^1/_4$ cup grated fresh ginger

grated zest of 1 lemon

20 ounces/560 g cream cheese

2 eggs

$^1/_4$ cup heavy cream

1 teaspoon vanilla essence

FOR THE CRUST

1 cup gingersnap cookie crumbs

2 tablespoons finely chopped crystallised ginger

2 tablespoons unsalted butter, melted and cooled

$^1/_4$ cup sugar

Preheat the oven to 325°F/170°C/Gas 3.

In a small saucepan over medium heat, combine water, sugar, fresh ginger and lemon zest. Bring to a simmer, stirring until the sugar is dissolved, then remove the ginger syrup from heat.

In the bowl of an electric mixer, beat the cream cheese on medium speed until smooth. Add the eggs, cream and vanilla essence and beat until smooth. Strain the ginger syrup through a fine-mesh sieve set over the bowl. Fold the syrup into cream cheese mixture until blended.

To make the crust, in a mixing bowl, combine the cookie crumbs, crystallised ginger, butter and $^1/_4$ cup sugar and stir until blended. Divide the crumb mixture among 4 mini-springform pans. With the back of a spoon, spread the crust mixture smoothly onto the bottom of each pan and divide the filling among the pans. Bake until the filling is set, about 15–18 minutes. Cool on racks to room temperature, then refrigerate at least 3 hours before serving.

Lemon Meringue Cake

Serves 6–8.

LEMON FILLING

1 cup milk

3^1/$_2$ ounces/100 g castor sugar

3 egg yolks

1 tablespoon cornflour

1 tablespoon plain flour

1^1/$_2$ ounces/40 g soft unsalted butter

^{1}/$_4$ cup lemon juice

4 ounces/110 g soft unsalted butter

^{1}/$_2$ cup castor sugar

1 tablespoon finely grated lemon rind

4 egg yolks

^{2}/$_3$ cup plain flour, sifted

1 teaspoon baking powder

^{1}/$_3$ cup milk

MERINGUE

4 egg whites

^{1}/$_4$ teaspoon cream of tartar

7 ounces/200 g castor sugar

For the lemon filling, heat the milk in a saucepan until nearly boiling, then remove from heat. Whisk the sugar, egg yolks, cornflour and plain flour in a bowl until the mixture is thick and pale. Gradually add the hot milk, stirring until the mixture is smooth, then return the mixture to the saucepan. Using a wooden spoon, stir the mixture continuously over medium heat until it boils and thickens, then remove from heat. Cool slightly, then stir in the butter and lemon juice. Cover closely with plastic wrap, cool to room temperature, then refrigerate until required.

Using an electric mixer, beat the butter, castor sugar and lemon rind until light and fluffy, then add the egg yolks, beating well after adding each. Add the sifted flour and baking powder alternately with milk and stir lightly until the mixture is smooth. Divide the mixture between two greased and floured 7^1/$_2$ inch/19 cm springform pans and set aside.

For the meringue, using an electric mixer, whisk the egg whites and cream of tartar until soft peaks form, then gradually add the sugar, whisking until the sugar dissolves and the mixture is thick and glossy. Divide the meringue between the cake pans, spreading it evenly over the cake batter. Bake the cakes at 350°F/180°C/Gas 4 for 35 minutes, then cool to room temperature. Just before serving, place one cake, meringue side up, on a large plate and spread evenly with chilled filling, then place the remaining cake, meringue side up, on top.

The cake is best served on the day it is made.

Northumberland, England

Rhubarb Cake

Serves 8–10.

1 pound/450 g trimmed rhubarb

8^1/$_4$ ounces/230 g golden castor sugar

finely grated zest and juice of 1 orange

7 ounces/200 g butter, softened

3 large eggs, beaten

8^1/$_4$ ounces/230 g self-raising flour, sifted

pinch of salt

3^1/$_2$ ounces/100 g ground almonds

Cut 10^3/$_4$ ounces/300 g rhubarb into chunks and toss with 2 ounces/50 g of the sugar, orange juice and 1 teaspoon of the orange zest. Set aside for 1 hour.

Cream the butter and remaining sugar until pale and light. Beat in the eggs a little at a time, adding a little flour if it starts to curdle. Beat in the remaining zest, then fold in the flour, salt and almonds.

Chop the remaining rhubarb and fold into the cake mixture with half the juices from the macerated rhubarb.

Preheat the oven to 350°F/180°C/Gas 4. Spoon the mixture into a buttered and lined 9 inch/23 cm tin and smooth down. Arrange the rhubarb on top, then spoon over the remaining juices. Bake for 1–1^1/$_4$ hours, protecting the top with foil if it is browning too much. Check with a skewer, then cool in the tin for at least 30 minutes before turning out.

Simon's Trifle

Since my school days, I have never enjoyed custard, but this trifle recipe is unique because of the zabaglione – just delicious!

sponge cake (packet or fresh)

wine (Cognac, Sherry, Cointreau or Tia Maria)

banana

mango

nuts

custard (packet)

zabaglione (recipe follows)

jelly

thick cream

chopped nuts

Line the base of a beautiful glass bowl with the sponge cake. Soak it generously with wine of choice.

Cover with a layer of banana, mango and nuts. Put a layer of custard on top. Cover that with homemade zabaglione.

Pour over a layer of jelly and top with a layer of whisked thick cream. Sprinkle the chopped nuts on top and add mango for decoration.

ZABAGLIONE

8 egg yolks

4 dessertspoons castor sugar

3 fl. ounces/90 ml Marsala

You'll need a medium-sized mixing bowl that will sit comfortably over a saucepan containing barely simmering water.

Into the mixing bowl place the egg yolks and sugar and start to whisk them (not on the heat yet) with an electric hand whisk or a balloon whisk until the mixture is pale and creamy – this will take about 4 minutes. Then gradually whisk in the Marsala bit by bit.

Now transfer the bowl to the saucepan – keep the heat very low – and continue whisking until the mixture thickens. This can sometimes be rather slow (10–15 minutes), but don't be tempted to turn the heat up because the mixture will curdle if it becomes too hot. It's better to keep the whisk in one hand and a crossword in the other, so you don't get too bored! When it does thicken, pour it into four warmed wine glasses and serve straightaway.

Rhubarb Cake

Cherry Clafoutis

Serves 6.

3 tablespoons sliced almonds

3 tablespoons unsalted butter, melted

$2/3$ cup all-purpose flour

$2/3$ cup plus 2 teaspoons sugar

$1/4$ teaspoon salt

4 large eggs

3 large egg yolks

$1 1/4$ cups heavy cream

1 vanilla bean, split and scraped

finely grated zest of 1 lemon

1 pound/450 g fresh, ripe cherries, stemmed and pitted

$1/4$ cup kirsch or brandy (optional)

Preheat the oven to 350°F/180°C/Gas 4. Place the sliced almonds in a single layer on a rimmed baking sheet. Toast until they are fragrant, about 5 minutes. Transfer to a wire rack to cool. Use 1 tablespoon melted butter to coat six $4 1/2$ x $1 3/4$ inch/$11 1/2$ x $4 1/2$ cm round baking dishes, and set aside.

Place the flour, $2/3$ cup sugar, salt and almonds in the bowl of a food processor fitted with the metal blade. Pulse until the mixture is finely ground. Transfer to a medium bowl. Add the eggs, egg yolks, $3/4$ cup cream, vanilla scrapings and lemon zest, and whisk to combine. Place in the refrigerator, and let rest for 30 minutes.

Place the cherries in a medium bowl. Add the kirsch, if using, and let it macerate for 30 minutes. Divide among the baking dishes. Whisk the remaining butter into the batter; pour the batter over cherries, and place the dishes on a rimmed baking sheet. Bake 20 minutes. Sprinkle with the remaining sugar, then bake until the tops are golden and bubbling, about 15 to 20 minutes. Transfer to a wire rack to cool.

Whip the remaining $1/2$ cup cream until soft peaks form. Serve warm or at room temperature topped with whipped cream.

Strawberry and Rose Petal Pavlova

Serves 4

9 ounces/250 g egg whites (from about 5–6 eggs)

13$^1/_2$ ounces/380 g sugar

$^1/_2$ teaspoon vanilla extract

2 teaspoons white wine vinegar

2 teaspoons cornflour

icing sugar

vanilla cream (recipe follows)

TO SERVE

2 punnets strawberries, quartered

pistachio praline (recipe follows)

rose petal syrup (recipe follows)

Preheat the oven to 325°F/170°C/Gas 3 and line a 13 x 9 inch/33 x 23 cm baking tray with baking paper.

In a bowl, beat the egg whites until stiff, then gradually beat in the sugar until the whites are thick and glossy. Fold in the vanilla, vinegar and cornflour. Spread onto the baking tray and bake for 20 minutes. Allow the meringue to cool on the tray for a few minutes.

Meanwhile, place a sheet of baking paper or a tea towel on a work surface, spread a piece of plastic wrap about the size of the meringue on top and dust with icing sugar. Carefully invert the meringue onto the plastic wrap and set aside to cool for 10 minutes.

Spread the vanilla cream over the meringue and, using the paper underneath to help, carefully roll the meringue lengthwise into a log shape (removing the paper as you roll). Wrap in plastic wrap, put on a tray and refrigerate for 3 hours.

To serve, cut the pavlova into 4 pieces and place on serving plates. Top with strawberries and pistachio praline and drizzle with rose petal syrup.

VANILLA CREAM

13$^1/_2$ fl. ounces/400 ml thickened cream

1 tablespoon icing sugar

1 vanilla bean, split

In a chilled bowl, whip the cream until firm peaks form. Fold in the icing sugar and scrape in the vanilla seeds. Cover and refrigerate until ready to use.

PISTACHIO PRALINE

1 cup castor sugar

$^1/_2$ cup water

1$^1/_2$ cups pistachio nuts

Line a large metal tray with baking paper. Place sugar in a saucepan, add half a cup of water and stir to dissolve, then boil over high heat until a golden caramel forms. Remove from heat, add pistachios and stir until the nuts are well coated. Spoon onto the prepared tray and set aside until the praline has hardened. Break into fine pieces. Store leftover praline in an airtight container.

ROSE PETAL SYRUP

2 cups castor sugar

4 cups water

1 cinnamon stick

2 tablespoons lemon juice

2 tablespoons rosewater

In a pan over medium heat, bring sugar, four cups water and cinnamon stick to the boil, then reduce heat and simmer for 5 minutes. Remove from heat and set aside. Once cool, stir in the lemon juice and rosewater. Set aside until ready to use.

Vanilla Cream Hearts with Raspberries and Blackberries

I first encountered this recipe in Sydney. It looks complicated to make but it is really very simple and the result is admired by all. A good eye-catcher for Valentine's Day, with the special heart shape and red raspberry sauce.

5 1/3 ounces/150 g vanilla mascarpone (recipe follows)

3 1/2 ounces/100 g cream cheese

4 1/2 ounces/125 g castor sugar

1 cup thick (45%) cream

1 cup thick plain yoghurt

9 ounces/250 g fresh raspberries

9 ounces/250 g fresh blackberries

6 tablespoons raspberry sauce (recipe follows)

Chill the bowl and blade of a food processor in the refrigerator. To make the cream hearts, blend the mascarpone, cream cheese and castor sugar in the food processor until smooth. Scrape the sides of the bowl with a plastic spatula occasionally to keep the mixture evenly distributed. Add the cream and yoghurt and blend briefly to incorporate.

Line 6 porcelain heart moulds with a double layer of wet muslin and carefully spoon in the cream mixture until the moulds are full and the surface is even. Put the moulds on a tray with a lip (to catch the whey), then cover with plastic film and refrigerate for at least 8 hours before serving.

To serve, arrange the raspberries and blackberries in the centre of each serving plate and spoon the raspberry sauce over the berries. Lift the cream hearts out of their moulds using the muslin, then invert each heart onto the berries and carefully remove the muslin. Serve immediately.

VANILLA MASCARPONE

2 limes

4 cups pouring (35%) cream

1 vanilla bean, split and scraped

1 scant teaspoon citric acid

Zest and juice the limes. Bring the lime zest, cream and vanilla bean to a vigorous boil in a deep stainless steel saucepan. Boil for 5 minutes until the cream separates.

Add the lime juice and citric acid to the cream mixture and bring it back to the boil. Simmer for 1 minute, then remove from the heat. Pour the cream through a fine-meshed sieve or muslin into a bowl. Put the bowl into the refrigerator until the mixture starts to set, about 5 hours.

Line a conical sieve with a double layer of wet muslin and position it over a 4 pint/2 litre plastic container. Pour the set cream into the sieve, then cover with plastic film and let it stand for 24 hours in the refrigerator to allow the whey to separate from the curd. Discard the whey and scoop the mascarpone from the sieve into a plastic container, then seal and refrigerate until ready to use. The mascarpone will keep for a week if refrigerated.

RASPBERRY SAUCE

18 ounces/510 g raspberries

3 1/3 fl. ounces/100 ml sugar syrup

1 fl. ounce/30 ml strained fresh lemon juice

Purée the raspberries with the sugar syrup and lemon juice in a food processor or blender. Pass the purée through a fine-meshed sieve and discard the seeds. Store the sauce in the refrigerator and use it within 3 days or the fruit will start to separate from the sugar. Whisk the sauce again just as you are about to serve it.

Toffee Caramel Bread and Butter Pudding

This is a hidden secret of a top hotel in Singapore. I have always loved the English version of bread and butter pudding but with toffee in the ingredients, this makes a sensational dish.

Serves 6-8.

EGG SAUCE

5 eggs

2 ounces/50 g sugar

2 cups milk

CARAMEL

7 ounces/200 g granulated sugar

1/2 cup water

PUDDING

1/2 cup raisins

2 ounces/50 g butter

18 slices white or brown bread, crustless (stale bread holds pudding together firmly)

First soak the raisins in boiling water just to make them fluffy, then set aside.

Meanwhile, prepare the egg sauce. Beat the eggs with the sugar until pale yellow, then slowly add the milk and whisk.

In another pan, melt the butter until golden brown.

In a separate pan, boil the granulated sugar with the water until golden brown or caramelised. Pour half of the caramel onto the baking dish. Spread to cover the entire bottom of the dish.

Pour some of the melted butter on the dish, then layer with the sliced bread. Pour some sauce over it, then sprinkle with some raisins. Continue the same procedure to make 3 layers of sliced bread.

Pour the remaining caramel over the bread. Bake in an oven preheated to 350°F/180°C/Gas 4 for 35–40 minutes.

Lemon and Elderflower Syllabub

Serves 6.

1 1/2 pounds/680 g blueberries

finely grated zest and juice of 2 lemons

1 1/4 cups elderflower cordial

FOR THE SYLLABUB

2 1/2 cups double cream

3 tablespoons elderflower cordial

finely grated zest of 2 lemons and juice of 1 lemon

2 large egg whites

2 ounces/50 g icing sugar, sieved

Put the blueberries into a bowl with the lemon zest, juice and elderflower cordial. Mix together thoroughly, cover the bowl and leave several hours or overnight.

For the syllabub, whip the cream with the elderflower cordial and the lemon juice, then stir in the zest. Take a clean whisk and beat the egg whites. When they are fairly stiff, whisk in the icing sugar a small amount at a time. Fold together the cream mixture and the whisked whites and leave to set for several hours.

To serve, divide the marinated blueberries between six large glasses, then heap the syllabub on top. Or you can serve them separately, with the syllabub piled in one bowl and the marinated blueberries in another.

Banff, Canada

CANADIAN RAIL RENAISSANCE

One of my many nicknames is "Amtrak Pooley", given to me by Annabelle Bond, because I simply love train rides. Of all the train rides I have experienced, none stands out more than the one run by the Canadian Pacific Railways – a five-day trip from Calgary to Banff, through the ruggedly beautiful Canadian Rockies in British Columbia. I was taking my mother on this adventure.

The ten carriages on the train meant there was plenty of room for everyone: all ten of us! No surprise then that the uniformed staff was able to devote their utmost attention to us from the very start, right up to the end of the journey. We were really transported in time to the turn of the century, with its old-style luxuries.

Our rail tour had been carefully planned to enable us to see everything even if the tracks did not extend to some places. We followed a convenient pattern: the train stopped at the exact spot where limousines or horse-drawn carriages awaited, we were taken to the attractions, then returned to the train for refreshing drinks.

We passed through places with intriguing names like Crowsnest and Kicking Bull Pass. These places are steeped in Native American folklore and history.

Canadian Mountie

In Head-Smashed-In Buffalo Jump, for example, Indians used to chase buffalo herds over precipices to kill them. One story relates how a brave was crushed by the falling buffalo as he watched the spectacle from a ledge under the cliff. The Crowsnest Pass was once a trading route for the Ktunaxa people and the building of the railway through their land had a great impact on their way of life.

We also went to the beautiful Lake Louise, a scenic area that is deservedly one of Canada's most popular tourist magnets.

As for food, we were pampered with the most succulent dishes imaginable, from eggs benedict to lobster thermidor… fine dining indeed! Lively conversation with the other guests enhanced a most enjoyable and memorable journey, one that was superlative in every sense of the word.

BEVERAGES & BETWEEN COURSES

Papua New Guinea

SURVIVING THE OVERLAND TREK IN TASMANIA
(OR HOW NOT TO COOK PANCAKES IN THE OUTBACK)

This is without a doubt one of my favourite cooking yarns… only it actually happened. I had formed, with five others, a trekking party to Tasmania. The plan was to hike 86 kilometres overland, from Cradle Mountain to Lake St Clair, travelling seven to eight hours a day for six days, cooking our own food and sleeping in tents. Unfortunately, what we didn't count on was our guide Wade underestimating the amount of provisions we would need. By day three we had run out of food. On the fourth day we shared one teabag between the six of us. The situation was becoming desperate and that night some of us dreamt of food. On day five, Wade had a brainwave. "I have pancake mixture," he announced, "but no oil!"

For those of you who have never cooked pancakes without oil, butter or lard, please don't bother trying. Between the six of us, we came up with different ways of making these pancakes without oil. We dropped the mixture into boiling water, we fried it, we tried scrambling it. We even steamed the mixture. Hunger pangs sharpened as hope of enjoying fresh, piping-hot pancakes quickly dimmed. That is, until Jane looked more closely at the label on the bottle of the foot balm she had just used to give herself a foot massage.

"Hey, what about trying my tea tree oil foot balm? It has 60 per cent butter in it!"

The men shook their heads at the idea and said "no way!" but I liked the sound of it.

Katharine trekking

So off I set on a new mission and cooked six perfect-smelling pancakes. There was just one tiny problem. On looking at the label on the bottle, it read: "Do not put anywhere near mucous membranes"!

We stared hungrily at those mouthwatering pancakes, speculating. Not for long. Within seconds, we were so hungry we were swallowing them down. And although we did spend the whole day imagining what might happen to us, in the end it was worth every bite.

So next time you go trekking in the Australian outback and forget the oil, just remember your foot balm. It does wonders for pancakes!

Christmas Grogg

Christmas is never Christmas without this gorgeous Grogg, which comes from Chicago. You can make it in advance and allow the aroma to permeate the house to create a warm Christmas feeling. Serve this piping hot with mince pies.

1 gallon/4^1/$_2$ litres port wine (Taylor)

1^1/$_2$ pints/710 ml bourbon (Jim Beam)

1^1/$_2$ pints/710 ml brandy

^{1}/$_4$ cup sugar, or less (taste as you add)

1 cup juice from dried fruit*

1 handful of whole almonds

Heat all the ingredients together. Do not boil. This should be served warm.

* Dried fruit juice includes apricots, apples, peaches, tangerines, almonds, ^{1}/$_2$ cup raisins, a few prunes, 2 cinnamon sticks, cinnamon seeds and whole cloves. Put in a 2 gallon/9 litre pot and cover with water. Simmer until almost mushy. Strain well. Serve warm.

Ginger Beer

My favourite drink and an old English classic – wonderful for summer. Serve with lots of ice and a sprig of mint.

2^2/$_3$ pounds/1^1/$_4$ kg sugar

5^1/$_4$ pints/2^1/$_2$ litres boiling hot water

2 tablespoons grated ginger

juice of 12 limes

5^1/$_4$ pints/2^1/$_2$ litres cold water

Add the sugar to boiling hot water and stir well. Add the grated ginger, followed by lime juice. Stir for 1 minute. Add cold water and stir well.

Pour the syrup into bottles or a barrel and close tightly. Keep this for 2 days.

After 2 days, strain the syrup and pour into bottle and keep tightly closed for 5–7 days to ferment.

After fermentation, place the bottles in a chiller.

Berry Fizz

Another of Liz Seaton's creations. Best served at Christmas parties and other celebrations. This is sweet, and guests should be warned of the alcohol content as it is highly potent!

Makes 30 glasses.

4 packets strawberry purée

4 pints/2 litres cranberry juice

2 pounds/910 g dark cherry juice

1 tablespoon sugar

3 bottles champagne

Mix the strawberry purée, cranberry juice and dark cherry juice, then add the sugar. Pour some berry mixture into the bottom of a champagne glass and fill the remainder with champagne. Makes a perfect Christmas or celebration drink.

Berry Fizz

Lyn Pooley's Elderflower Cordial

This is undoubtedly my favourite drink recipe that reminds me of Felden, our home in England. Lyn would pick the elderflower heads from the garden and make gallons of this syrup for the summer months. Simply delicious.

60 heads elderflowers

4 fl. ounces/120 ml citric acid

$6^2/_3$ pounds/3 kg sugar

4 lemons, halved and squeezed

6 pints/3 litres cold boiled water

Elderflower can only be found in the countryside of England. Put all the elderflower heads and the remaining ingredients into a bucket, then mix and stir. Leave the mixture for 2 days, stirring occasionally. Strain well into a

Polynesia

bottle. Lyn always used an old-fashioned nappy to do this, but cheesecloth works well too. This liquid should be used in a similar fashion to a cordial diluted with water.

Lyn Pooley's Elderflower Champagne

1 gallon/$4^1/_2$ litres cold water

$1^1/_4$ pounds/560 g sugar

7 heads elderflowers

2 lemons

2 tablespoons white wine vinegar

Boil the water and pour over the sugar. When cold, throw in the flowers, sliced lemons and add the vinegar. Leave for 24 hours. Strain and keep in strong bottles. Cork well.

Lyn Pooley's Lemon Squash

3 lemons

1 fl. ounce/30 ml citric acid

2 pounds/910 g granulated sugar

1 pint/$^1/_2$ litre water

Slice the lemons thinly, and put them into a bowl with the citric acid and sugar. Pour on the boiling water and stir until the sugar has completely dissolved. Leave to stand overnight. Bottle and keep in the fridge. Serve as a cordial

Cucumber Sorbet

When cooking a six-course meal for entertaining clients or important guests I always serve a sorbet to refresh the palate before serving the main course. This sorbet is a favourite and comes from Huka Lodge in New Zealand. The sweet combination of the cucumber with the mint leaves a refreshing taste to give you the extra pace to continue with the main course!

1 medium-sized cucumber, skinned and seeded

juice of 1 lemon

$^1/_2$ teaspoon finely chopped mint

$^4/_5$ cup syrup

Place the cucumber in a liquidiser and process until smooth. Pass through a fine sieve into a clean bowl, pushing as much of the pulp through as possible. Add all the other ingredients and mix together.

Pour into a sorbetiere and process, or place in a large bowl in the freezer, whisking regularly to achieve a smooth texture.

Serve in a chilled glass or cucumber boats with a sprig of fresh mint.

Mangosteen Sorbet

Mangosteen Sorbet

Another perfect idea for a sorbet. Mangosteens can sometimes be very sweet so buy the slightly under-ripe ones.

1 cup sugar

3 cups water

juice of half a lemon

5 mangosteens

Combine the sugar with the water in a saucepan, then boil for 15 minutes into a light syrup. Cool, then add the lemon juice, and set aside.

Open the mangosteens, then scoop out the seeds with the pulp. Mix with $1/2$ cup of sugar mixture, and push through a strainer with a spoon. Squeeze out as much pulp as you can, leaving the seeds. Discard the seeds.

Mix the mangosteen pulp with the remaining sugar syrup. Transfer into a plastic box with enough space to stir the sorbet, and freeze. Then stir twice every two hours. Leave in the freezer overnight or until needed.

Lychee Sorbet

Serves 4.

1 can (1 pound/450 g) lychees

4 ounces/110 g granulated sugar

2 tablespoons lemon or lime juice

2 egg whites

thinly pared rind of 1 lime, to decorate

Drain the syrup from the lychees into a jug and make up to 8 fl. ounces/240 ml with cold water. Place in a pan and add sugar. Heat gently to dissolve the sugar, then bring to the boil. Simmer without stirring for 10 minutes. Remove from heat and leave to cool slightly.

Purée the lychees in a liquidiser or press through a sieve. Mix the purée with the syrup and lemon or lime juice. Pour into a shallow freezer container and freeze for 1-2 hours, or until almost frozen.

Whisk the egg whites until fairly stiff. Cut the frozen mixture into small pieces and work in a food processor to break down the crystals. Do not let the mixture melt; quickly incorporate the beaten egg white, then pour into slightly deeper freezer container. Return to the freezer until firm.

Blanch the lime rind in boiling water for 2 minutes, then drain and refresh in cold water. Cut into thin strips.

Ten minutes before serving, scoop the sorbet into individual glass dishes and decorate with lime rind.

Lychee Sorbet

Katharine Pooley has been travelling since the day she was born, and her fascination for cooking started when she was only 5 years old. She has now travelled extensively to over 120 countries and attended several top cookery colleges, namely Cordon Bleu and Prue Leith. What started as a hobby of collecting recipes as memories from each country has grown into a large collection of unique dishes from all over the world. She has now decided to share these souvenirs in a personalised travel cookbook.

Katharine was educated in Oxfordshire and went to university in France. She has spent the last 12 years living in Hong Kong, where she worked for Morgan Stanley and Barclays Bank. She has also lived in Vietnam, Singapore, Bahrain and London.

Apart from being passionate about her travels and cooking, she loves sports, mountains, interior decorating and animals, particularly her four dogs. Her future plans for next year have led her to apply to a veterinary course and she plans to open her own boutique in London, specialising in exclusive homeware. Her dream and aspiration is to climb Mount Everest one day.

When she is not travelling around the world, Katharine divides her time between Asia, London and particularly Scotland, where she believes her true heart lies.

Fishtail Mountain, The Himalayas, Nepal